INDEPENDENT
BIBLE STUDY

INDEPENDENT BIBLE STUDY

Using the
ANALYTICAL CHART
and the
INDUCTIVE METHOD

by IRVING L. JENSEN

MOODY PRESS
CHICAGO

Moody Press, a ministry of the Moody Bible Institute, is
designed for education, evangelization and edification.
If we may assist you in knowing more about Christ and
the Christian life, please write us without obligation to:
Moody Press, c/o MLM, Chicago, Illinois 60610.

Printed in the United States of America

To
My Mother and Father
who
loved their children to the Lord

"In truth thou canst not read the Scriptures too much;
And what thou readest, thou canst not read too well;
And what thou readest well, thou canst not too well understand;
And what thou understandest well, thou canst not too well teach;
And what thou teachest well, thou canst not too well live."

—MARTIN LUTHER

PREFACE

DISCOVERY—ENJOYMENT—SHARING: these are the reasons for this book.

My eyes were first opened to the true and full delights of methodical firsthand study of the Bible while studying at seminary under others whose enthusiasm for the Word was contagious. Dr. Emily Werner, Dr. Howard T. Kuist and Professor Robert Traina were some of my inspirers. The latter two have expressed their thoughts in books from which has come the inspiration for this present work, with its different purpose.

It was while teaching Bible analysis at a Bible school, and later at a college, that I had the pleasant and rewarding experience of expanding the graphic method used by my former teachers and of training students in this method of independent Bible study. Now, after these years of developing and refining, with hundreds of students as "guinea pigs," the time seems ripe for fulfilling the request of many who have wanted to have a description of the method in print, as well as for introducing the method to a wider audience.

I have used the analytical chart method in Sunday schools, young people's meetings, midweek Bible studies, and in hosts of sermon preparations. Its other applications are numerous. There is no Bible student—of laity or clergy—to whom the message of these pages is irrelevant. It is sincerely hoped that through these pages the reader will become more convinced of the need for methodical independent study, and that the seeds of suggestions sown herewith will reap fruitful Biblical knowledge in his life.

I am deeply grateful to all who have had any part in the production of this work. I am especially grateful to my wife, Charlotte, for the many hours given to the typing of the manuscript in the midst of home responsibilities.

I. L. J.

TABLE OF CONTENTS

LIST OF CHARTS AND ILLUSTRATIONS

INTRODUCTION

THE FRUITS OF BIBLE STUDY are largely determined by *how* the Bible is studied.

There are various approaches to Bible study, just as there are various ways of studying the great paintings at an art gallery. One student makes only a hurried, casual visit to the gallery, deciding to spend most of his time reading what others have seen in the art works. The second student does incomparably better. He spends a long time in each hall as he lets the artists speak for themselves. But he errs in refusing to read the captions, to listen to the guides, or to inquire into the life of the artist. The third student goes one step further. He recognizes that although this study is *his* study, and should, therefore, be firsthand, yet helps—for example, a guide's description of the background of an oil painting—can amplify and enrich that study.

The term "independent Bible study" as used in these pages is not intended to suggest an independent attitude of self-sufficiency or vanity where all outside help is disdained and ignored. The core of one's study should be of an *original firsthand* character, but wherever possible a selective and well-timed reference to supplementary aids is desirable. In some cases, few or no aids are available to the student, as in the case of the missionary on the jungle trail. It should be encouraging to such a one that the unavailability of aids is not a serious handicap to his study. For those who have the aids, and use them, there should never develop a dependency on them which is either total or automatic like a lame man leaning on a crutch.

The Bible should be a very personal companion for everyone. God intends that *all* should read and study it—laity as well as clergy, young as well as old. This universal intent is borne out by the perspicuous content of the Bible (consider the child's amazing grasp of Biblical truths!); by the original production of the Bible (e.g., the New Testament was originally written in the common, universal language of that day); by the history of the Scriptures' worldwide distribution; and by the applicability of the Bible to the everyday life of the man on the street.

It is true that some are called to fields of specialization or concentration in Biblical studies. The Christian Church is indebted to these for such contributions as textual research—the threefold task of determining as accurately as possible what the *words* of the original writings must have been, what was the intended *meaning* of such words, and what *vernacular* words would faithfully translate that meaning. The Church is indebted to others for their research in history, geography and local customs of the Bible lands and in many other vital areas of Biblical fact. Actually, these contributions in the specialized fields make "laboratory analysis" possible for the Bible student. They supply some of the tools and instruments. They provide the reference library. They offer technical assistance when needed. On these the Bible student is dependent—very dependent.

But the analysis of the Bible passage is still the student's problem, or project. Bible study is an *individual* task, incumbent upon all Christians. It behooves each child of God to *grow personally* in the knowledge of God's Word, and one of the first steps in this progressive growth is that of becoming an independent student of the Bible.

The learning of a method of Bible study which stresses the independence described above imparts a self-confidence and zeal without which Bible study could become a chore. The author sincerely hopes that the following pages will help to represent independent study as attractive and vital as it really is.

THE BIBLE, YOUR EYES, AND A PENCIL

The triad of *Bible, eye,* and *pencil* represents three crucial factors in a fruitful study engagement of the Christian: the Bible, because of all written records it is the unique clue to an abundant Christian life; the eyes, because the Bible is not merely to be owned, or respected, or occasionally referred to, but to be read, and reread, and scrutinized, and studied, with the physical and spiritual eyes; the pencil, because as far as the mental abilities are concerned, nothing crystallizes or makes permanent or helps one's remembering, as does *writing down* the things studied.

The Bible. The dearth of Bible study in the Christian church is alarming. This dearth can be traced to various sources. In the average Christian home, family devotions with Bible reading are fast passing off the scene, so that many of our youth are not recognizing the Book as the spring of life, worthy of a lifetime of study. Then also, there is no time for personal Bible study in one's week. Every week night is taken up with clubs, circles, committee meetings, parties, engagements of all sorts. Plainly, the average Christian is too busy committeeing or clubbing. Some things must go, and Bible study is one of them.

Spirituality and Bible study in the Christian church go hand in hand. Spirituality cannot be driven into a man, for it involves hunger. The church may invite the Christian to the spiritual banquet, offer a well-balanced and wholesome menu, provide attractive atmosphere and efficient service, but if the man is not hungry he will not eat. In physical hunger, the body wonderfully knows its need, and so craves food. For spiritual hunger, the Christian must know he is in need. He must know that he needs to grow in grace, to please his Saviour, to be aware of the demands of the Word, to know what his heritage is in Christ, to appropriate the strength and power which God offers, to recognize the devices of Satan, and to interpret the times in which he lives. If the Christian knows these are among his greatest needs and that the Bible not only identifies these needs but also meets them, he will hunger for this Word. There is no abnormality about being a serious Bible student. In God's eyes it is most normal because it is most necessary.

Your Eyes. The appeal to use one's physical eyes in the reading and analyzing of the Bible under the illuminating light of the Holy Spirit has as its ultimate end *spiritual perception*. The difference between mere seeing and deeper perceiving is remarkably illustrated in the empty tomb narrative of John 20:1-10, where three different words for "see" are used in the Greek text. Upon receiving Mary Magdalene's report that Jesus' body has been taken out of the sepulcher, Peter and John run together to the sepulcher. John, who arrives first, does not enter, but stoops down and, looking in, "sees (*blepei*) the linen clothes lying" (v. 5). This was the mere *viewing* of the facts from without, apparently without any significant reaction other than the affirmation that what Mary had reported was true. Peter's observing was more intimate, for he went *into* the sepulcher, and "beholdeth" (*theorei*) clearly something astounding: the napkin, or head roll, was still intact like a cocoon, all rolled up (vv. 6-7). Peter's beholding was more intense than John's viewing, for Peter was face to face with the impossible: the separation of a body from its grave wrappings, without the disturbance of the latter. By this time, John also entered the sepulcher, "and he perceived (*eiden*), and believed" (v. 8). John's reaction was that of *perception* that here was the impossible, and, further, that God had done the impossible. And he believed.

John's first viewing was from a distance and therefore inadequate. When he entered into the innermost recesses of the chamber itself, he not only saw facts but perceived their significance and solution.

Analytical study of the Bible is intended to lead the student into the innermost chambers of the Book for spiritual perception, involving the impossible, the incomprehensible, the supernatural, and the eternal.

A Pencil. The extra step in Bible study of writing down what one studies may seem to some to be hardly worth the effort. However, when viewed from the standpoint that effective Bible study is methodical Bible study, and that methodical Bible study invariably involves writing of some sort, then a graphic method of study intended to develop such methodical study is worthy of serious consideration. In a very real sense the pencil so methodically used becomes another eye to the student, to capture more of the Biblical truth with greater clarity.

THE NEED FOR METHODICAL BIBLE STUDY

Men reject or neglect the challenge of Bible study either because the Bible is too small, or because it is too big.

To the unbeliever, the Bible is too small. It is just another book (though its excellence may be granted) describing the philosophies and experiences of men and nations in bygone eras, of no more value to men today than any good history or philosophy book. To the one with such a view of Scripture, the Bible is too small for him to become overly concerned about "analyzing" it.

To many believers, whose hearts by nature crave spiritual help from some source, the Bible looms too big for a serious undertaking in the study of its thousand-plus pages. The would-be student is overwhelmed by the problems: Where do I begin? How much do I study at a time? What does it say? What does it mean? How can I efficiently study? How can I remember what I have studied? This seemingly impassable mountain of problems is often bypassed or skirted via short Bible reading or mere occasional reference to familiar passages. In some cases, a defeated Christian will encamp himself at the foot of the mountain and live the rest of his life in a meager, restricted existence.

The problems of Bible study listed above will always exist, as long as there is a Bible being studied. But they need not appear as an impassable mountain. For the Christian who has committed his life to Christ unreservedly, who opens his heart daily to the illuminating ministry of the Holy Spirit and sincerely wants to study the Bible, the clue to the conquering of the mountain is probably to be found in a practical and fruitful *method* of study.

* * *

Method is simply *orderly procedure.* It works with the given materials, proceeds according to principles and rules, aims at a completion, and honors such qualities as patience, deliberation, objectivity, subjectivity, and toil and sweat. During the actual undertaking of methodical Bible study the end may not always be distinguished from the beginning, but because the student has acquired a sufficient measure of confidence which attends methodicalness in study, he continues to labor in his study, because he knows that the lines of methodical study will eventually converge at the goal's point.

This writer once had impressed upon him the necessity of method in the common task of landscaping. Having built a house on the side of a hill, and having used the services of the bulldozer as much as the steep grading would allow, he took upon himself the manual phase of the landscaping. The property sloped two ways: north-south, and east-west, which demanded a complicated system of terraces and slopes. Every slope had been surveyed, and a master plan for the finished grounds had been drawn. The total job involved relocating yards of dirt, digging, building walls and rock gardens, constructing drainage channels and sidewalks, planting trees, bushes, and grass.

During the first days of labor, the sweat and toil were forgotten in the newness and excitement of the project. But then came the moment of sober evaluation of the actual weight of a wheelbarrow of dirt, of the foot-pounds of energy involved in moving boulders, of the long hours of wall building—all of this yet to be accomplished. Natural reaction said, "It can *never* be done." Desperation said, "It *has* to be done." Logic and reasoning said, "If it is ever done, it will be by *methodical* deliberate work." This was the only solution, for by itself, each terrace and wall and slope was an individual project, the construction of which was surely within the realm of possibility. And since each smaller project was part of the master plan, there was no fear of wasted or incongruous labors. The whole was seen to be attainable because it was the sum of its attainable parts. The will and strength put themselves to the tasks in line with the method until eventually the task was accomplished.

So it is with serious Bible study. By using a method or methods, rather than haphazardly dabbling in the books, the student acknowledges the dimensions of his task, is motivated to pursue to its conclusion the task which he undertakes, proceeds by orderly units and according to acceptable rules and principles, and eventually accomplishes that for which he strives.

There are many methods of Bible study. Howard Vos, in his book *Effective Bible Study*,[1] describes seventeen different approaches in studying the Bible. Actually, some methods of study involve more than one approach. Also, there may be many applications of one method. It is the intention of this work to present the *inductive method* of study, as it is applied in *Bible analysis*, through the graphic construction of

[1]Howard Vos, *Effective Bible Study* (2d ed., Grand Rapids: Zondervan Publishing House, 1956).

an *analytical chart*. Actually then, a composite of three methods is presented: inductive method, analytical method, and chart method.

Since the inductive method presented in these chapters is based on the recognition of the books of the Bible as compositional units of literature, it is the purpose of chapter one to orient the student to this basic concept, and to make him structure-conscious, aware of the "togetherness" of units of study in the Bible. Chapter two then proceeds to define and describe the inductive method of Bible analysis, and to indicate why it is valued so highly as a study method.

The inductive method has been profitably applied in various manners. Working from suggestions first received from his teachers at The Biblical Seminary in New York, the writer has found it a very fascinating experience in his years of teaching to develop and teach a graphic analytical chart method, which is minutely described in chapters three and four.

No one method of study proposes to be the magic wand in the hard discipline of Bible study. The student of the Bible would do well to acquaint himself with, and use, many methods of study. Even in the use of one method the procedures should not be so ironclad that freedom of thought and expression is inhibited. All too easily one can be led unconsciously into a rut, bound to a pattern. Such suppression can become a long drawn-out situation, as illustrated by the sign at a muddy road which read: "Choose your rut—you'll be in it for the next forty miles."

The methodical student's goal could not be higher—that of a better knowledge of the eternal Word of God. In a very real sense he is a Bible scholar, taught by holy men of God who spoke as they were moved by the Holy Ghost. As Bible scholar, it is his task to see the FACTS amid APPEARANCES. The task is hard and, as one has observed, "he plies the slow, unhonored and unpaid task of observation."[2] But when the observation brings forth obedient response and action, with its attendant blessing, the task is seen to be an exceedingly glorious one.

[2]Ralph W. Emerson, quoted in Charles Eberhardt, *The Bible in the Making of Ministers* (New York: Association Press, 1949), p. 127.

INDEPENDENT
BIBLE STUDY

CHAPTER I

THE BIBLE AS LITERATURE

ONE OF THE UNIQUE CHARACTERISTICS of the Scriptures, in view of the diverse human authorship, is its oneness or unity of message. This unity is appropriately reflected in the singular noun "Bible." Historically the title was not always singular, for in the early days of the Church Greek-speaking Christians referred to the entire group of Old and New Testament books as *Ta Biblia,* "the books." The Latins borrowed the word *biblia* but translated it in the singular, and from this Latin word has come our English singular "Bible."

Much has been written on the overall unity and purposeful design of this literary masterpiece. F. F. Bruce has rightly observed that this unity was not attained through the selectivity of an anthologist in compiling books of similar nature, but that "somehow or other it [the Bible] *grew* in the course of these many centuries until at length it attained full stature as the Bible which we know."[1] Erich Sauer refers to the Scriptures as "a skillfully constructed building, the ground plan of which was prepared in advance, and of the whole of which Christ is the end, a system with measure and proportion, in which each separate part is organically incorporated as a member of the whole."[2] One often speaks of the crimson thread of atonement that is woven into the entire garment of the Scriptures, determining the pattern of history, biography, testimony, and doctrine. The Bible is unquestionably a unity of revelation, internally

[1]F. F. Bruce, *The Books and the Parchments* (Westwood, N. J.: Fleming H. Revell Co., 1950), p. 87.
[2]Erich Sauer, *From Eternity to Eternity* (London: The Paternoster Press, 1954), p. 116.

27

evidencing a supernatural inspiration of its writing and a supernatural superintendence in the preservation and canonization of its integral parts.

I. STRUCTURAL STUDY: A PRIORITY

While the Bible is in many respects a literary unity, it more correctly can be said to comprise *individual literary works,* and each of these individual books normally constitutes a unit of study.

Recognizing the structural characteristics of a Biblical book is not a side-path journey that can be deleted from one's study itinerary. God has been pleased to communicate to mankind a revelation of Himself in the form of literature, and "a clear grasp of the outer literary form is an essential guide to the inner matter and spirit."[3]

Whether the Biblical author is composing a biographical sketch, a historical epic, or a logical discourse, he can never include everything that might be said on the subject. Instead, he is inspired to *select* only that which will accomplish the purpose at hand and to arrange such selected material in the order that will best suit that purpose. The results are varied. In some cases, as is true of parts of Jeremiah, the chronological sequence intentionally is not followed. Mark may choose to place two incidents next to each other in his composition, although a comparison with the other synoptic Gospels may reveal a span of six full days of activity as intervening between the events. The literary structure may or may not follow a chronological sequence, but in any case it is determined by the author's *selectivity,* not by such standards as exhaustiveness and sequence—as worthy as they are in themselves. Any analysis of a composition, e.g., historical analysis, is based on the text itself, which includes the literary structure of that text. A full-orbed Bible study, therefore, commences with this structural study.

[3]Richard G. Moulton, *The Literary Study of the Bible* (London: Ibisler and Co., Ltd., 1905), p. vi.

II. CONTENT AND FORM

The substance of a book of the Bible is basically twofold: (1) units of materials, or *content,* and (2) relations between those units, or *form.* A book, in a wide sense of the term, may contain both of these and not be a literary work. For example, a telephone directory contains materials (names of subscribers) and relations between these materials (alphabetical order of names). But it is obvious that a telephone directory is not a literary work.

Form is the key to locked treasures of the content of the book. Just as recognizing the alphabetical order of names in a telephone directory is the key to its use, so form recognition is a necessary key to the understanding of a Biblical book. Henry O. Taylor has stated that "art is not spontaneous, but carefully intended; no babbling of a child, but a mutual fitting of form and content, in which efficient unison the artist's intellect has worked."[4] Biblical composition demonstrates structural order, the order which Milton describes as "Heaven's first law."

A Christian who studies a book of the Bible with serious intentions must learn its facts by way of its form, or, stated another way, he must learn its teaching by way of its structural context. For maximum profit he cannot study some parts and overlook others, as though he were selecting the most lustrous jewels from the store counter and refusing others. Rather, he will consider the total message of the Book as likened to a beautiful living plant, through *all* parts of which flows a stream of *life.* To him the roots, the fruits, the stems, and the leaves all have their individual functions in the one plant, a living specimen of the creative hand of God.

Form or structure may therefore be said to involve all of the relations and interrelations which bind terms into a

---

[4]Henry O. Taylor, *The Mediaeval Mind,* I, 20, quoted by Robert Traina, *Methodical Bible Study* (privately published, 1952), p. 37.

literary unit. To observe that there is an underlying design in the scriptural writings, upon which and about which words are built, is to recognize that the factor of purposive selectivity was basic to the work of the Biblical writers, as they were inspired by God.

Each version of the Bible attempts to give some help to the student in recognizing the more obvious aspects of form, such as identification of *units* of thought. For instance, the Authorized Version presents the Scriptures in units of chapters, each chapter presumably intended to convey one main thought. In the same version each chapter is divided into one-verse paragraphs. Actually, the original Biblical manuscripts were written without such divisions, mainly to conserve space. Our chapter divisions were originated by Stephen Langton, in his edition of the Latin Vulgate of 1228. The verse divisions are traced back to Robert Stephanus' Geneva Edition of 1551. Nine years later, in the Geneva version of 1560, each verse was made a separate paragraph.

The locations of some of Langton's chapter divisions are unfortunately misplaced, at times prematurely ending a unit of thought. Of course, the chapter (and verse) divisions are fixed and unalterable, and only format clues within the text (such as the *American Standard Version's* paragraph format) or the student's own discernment will identify the misplaced divisions. The list of segment units of study as given in some examples in Appendix I suggests where some chapter divisions could have been more appropriately placed.

The most obvious difference as to format between most King James versions and such modern versions as the New International, Revised Standard, and Berkeley, is that for the latter the paragraph is made up of a group of verses, whereas the King James Version presents each verse as a separate paragraph. The advantages of the larger paragraph format will be cited later in this study.

III. STRUCTURAL UNITY

Any literary work, being a unity, may be said to have been constructed about one basic structural framework. This underlying structure, on closer scrutiny, is made up of units of composition related to each other and related to the whole unity. The same applies to the Bible. Each book of the Bible is a compositional unity comprising interrelated segments which are themselves compositional units and, therefore, appropriate study units. The application of this literary principle to the books of the Bible is basic to the method of study suggested in the present work.

A. Some Pertinent Observations

Since the application of the above-mentioned literary principles to the books of the Bible may appear to be an unrealistic generalization, certain observations and explanations are pertinent at this point.

1. It is very obvious that liberal higher criticism rejects the unity of most of the Biblical books, e.g., Isaiah, Micah, Nahum, Habbakuk, Zephaniah, and Haggai. It is to be observed, however, that in utilizing form as a tool for determining authorship, form critics have denied the very liberties which an author may take in creating a literary work. A typical scholarly defense of the unity of an entire book is Oswald T. Allis' *The Unity of Isaiah,* which is a classic in its field.

2. Not only did the Holy Spirit move the Biblical writers to speak words per se, but He also moved them to speak such words within the framework of a reflective pattern, evidencing logic, beauty, force, etc. Merrill C. Tenney, in writing on the "genius" of the Gospels, asserts that the basic presupposition of his approach is that "the content, *form* and doctrine of the Gospels are the product of the Holy Spirit,

to whom they owe their vital power."[5] Robert Girdlestone, who has contributed much in the field of word studies, has underscored the importance of contextual study in the determination of intended meanings of individual words:

> The opinion formerly held by some scholars, that all Hebrew words are equivocal, is now generally regarded as an exaggeration, and, although there are differences of opinion as to the meaning of some words, the dictionaries of such men as Gesenius and Furst, being the embodiment of Jewish tradition confirmed and checked by investigations into cognate languages, give us a fair general idea of the meaning of the roots. This however, is not enough. . . . The exact shade of meaning of each Hebrew word can be ascertained only by an induction of instances leading to a definite conception of the sacred usage in each case.[6]

3. To proceed from the contention of the unity of an entire book of the Bible to that of the unity of segments within the whole is not an illogical or rash step. If the individual books are units of composition, even though of varying literary quality, what is normally claimed for any work of literature may be claimed for a Biblical book, namely, that the parts have structure as well as does the whole.

4. It is evident that the books of the Bible do not all have the same structure. Prophetic books, while generally setting forth similar messages concerning sin, judgment, mercy, and deliverance, vary as to methods of treatment, proportions given to the Messianic hope, and locations of climax, if any. It is also very evident that some books are more "literary," in the strict definition of the term, than are others. The Epistle to the Hebrews and the First Epistle of Peter are generally regarded as being highly literary works, and this is at least partly confirmed by the fact that the meanings

[5]Merrill C. Tenney, *The Genius of the Gospels* (Grand Rapids: Wm. B. Eerdmans Publishing Co., 1951), p. 10. Italics mine.

[6]Robert Baker Girdlestone, *Synonyms of the Old Testament* (Grand Rapids: Wm. B. Eerdmans Publishing Co., 1953), p. 6.

of much of their vocabulary are derived from a lexicon of classical Greek, which was the language of the litterateur. Luke's Gospel is also cited as an example of one of the more literary compositions. Howard Kuist makes this appraisal of Luke:

> The Gospel according to Luke is the most artistically arranged of our four Gospels and deserves Renans' encomium, "The most beautiful book ever written."[7]

Regarding the New Testament books of lesser literary quality, such as some of the very personal epistles, some scholars follow the extreme position of denying any literary quality whatever, a view which, in its modern form, originated with Adolph Deissmann. This noted German scholar was one of the pioneers working with the papyri findings of the last decades of the nineteenth century in demonstrating that the Greek of the New Testament was the Koine Greek, or the common language of everyday life. H. E. Dana and Julius R. Mantey, while recognizing the monumental contributions of Deissmann, and while agreeing that the New Testament Greek is not a "language of the Holy Ghost," nevertheless maintain that there is a distinction between Koine Greek and the Greek of the New Testament. They write:

> Still it is true that there is a place in philological science for the term "Biblical Greek." This would be true for the one fact alone of the distinctive literature of transcendant (sic) interest which composes it. It is also true that the New Testament and Septuagint present a distinctive type of the Koine. They are superior in literary quality to the average presented by the papyri, and yet do not exhibit the classical aim of the Atticistic writers.[8]

[7]Howard Tillman Kuist, *These Words Upon Thy Heart* (Richmond: John Knox Press, 1947), p. 104.
[8]H. E. Dana and Julius R. Mantey, *A Manual Grammar of the Greek New Testament* (New York: The Macmillan Co., 1950), pp. 10, 11.

Further, it is observed that some Biblical books *appear* to lack a structural pattern, with verses and segments listed unsequentially and in apparent isolation. For instance, some hold that the unit of thought in Proverbs is one verse,[9] and that an integrated outline of such personal epistles as I Timothy is difficult to ascertain.[10] Unquestionably, diversity is one of the obvious characteristics of the structure of the books of the Bible.

Variety of literary types of the Biblical books also accounts for this diversity. Richard G. Moulton refers to the two basic kinds of writing, namely poetry (creative), and prose (discussion of what exists), either of which can be descriptive (author's words throughout) or presentative (author nowhere appears). Poetic writings are either epic, lyric, or drama, depending on whether they are mainly description, reflection, or action, respectively. Prose writings are either history, philosophy, or rhetoric, also depending on whether they are mainly description, reflection, or action, respectively. These definitions are illustrated in the following chart, which has been adapted from Moulton's work, *The Literary Study of the Bible.*[11] The books of the Bible are listed in the classification which identifies the major contents of each book. The Old Testament prophets, representing a combination of types, have been included under history, philosophy, and rhetoric. A glance at the distribution of literary types in the Bible confirms the variety of styles confronting the student in the library called *The Holy Bible.*

B. The Search for Structure

Every honest student should desire above all to let the Holy Writ speak for itself. This is the only fair and natural

[9]See Merrill F. Unger, *Introductory Guide to the Old Testament* (Grand Rapids: Zondervan Publishing House, 1951), p. 372.
[10]Merrill C. Tenney, *The New Testament* (Grand Rapids: Wm. B. Eerdmans Publishing Co., 1955), p. 349.
[11]Op. cit., p. 78.

DESCRIPTIVE
(AUTHOR'S WORDS THROUGHOUT)

POETRY (CREATIVE)	**EPIC** Parts of Wisdom Literature	**MAINLY DESCRIPTION** ↑	**HISTORY** Genesis through Esther Gospels and Acts Prophets Revelation
	LYRIC Psalms Song of Solomon Prophets	**REFLECTION**	**PHILOSOPHY** Prophets N. T. Epistles	**PROSE** (RECOUNTING)
	DRAMA Job	**MAINLY ACTION** ↓	**RHETORIC** Deuteronomy N. T. Epistles Revelation Prophets

PRESENTATIVE
(AUTHOR NOWHERE APPEARS)

LITERARY TYPES of BIBLICAL LITERATURE

approach to any writing. In such an approach to the Bible, two questions constantly face the student: What does God say? and, How does He say it? The second question, involving form or structure, is as important as the first.

What B. B. Warfield wrote concerning the study of the Bible as a whole applies equally to the study of an individual book of the Bible:

> . . . we must approach the Book as a whole with our eyes open to the relations borne by part to part,—their chronological order, their mutual interdependencies and interrelations, their several places in the advancing delivery of doctrine, in the development of Christian life, in the elaboration of Church organization and worship,—in order that

we may understand the method of God in creating His Church through the labors of these apostolic writers.[12]

The mutual interrelations of the segments within a book must ever be recognized as unfolding the mind of the true author, God. One does not inject a magical strain into the scriptural compositions by recognizing this divine authorship behind the human authorship. On the other hand, the very fact of such a unique authorship is basis for expecting in the writings themselves, and in the structure thereof, an element of the "supra-natural," transcending what human authorship without the divine inspiration could compose.

This uniqueness of the pattern or structure of the scriptural compositions is also deduced from the analogy of God's creative hand in natural revelation. The minutest details of the creation, which is the divine revelation in nature, point to a creation of beauty and order in *substance* as well as in *relationships*. Even so, special revelation is its own witness to the divine creation of the original writing, unique and infallible as to individual words, and purposefully planned as to structure.

Motivated by such a conviction of this unique structure of the Biblical compositions, the earnest Bible student will diligently apply himself not only to the study of isolated parts, but will search for those relationships between the parts as clues to what God intended to reveal. Such has been the experience of many Bible students. J. Albrecht Bengel, in relating his study of the maxims of Proverbs, says,

I have often been in such an attitude of soul, that those chapters in the Book of Proverbs in which I had before looked for no connection whatever, presented themselves

[12]B. B. Warfield, Introductory Note, in John H. Kerr, *An Introduction to the Study of the Books of the New Testament* (New York: Fleming H. Revell Co., 1931), p. xv.

to me as if the proverbs belonged in the most beautiful order one with another.[13]

Robert D. Culver has recorded his experience with the Book of Daniel thus:

> The writer gave much time to study of the Book of Daniel over a period of several years without discerning the crucial importance of the structure of the book to an accurate interpretation of it. I am now quite convinced that the almost indispensable key to the book is the structure. This structure is at once the most obvious and elusive feature of the book.[14]

Two typical units of study illustrate the necessity of studying structure and relationships for clues to a fuller apprehension of the Word's intents. Matthew 1:1-17 records the genealogy of Jesus Christ. The structure of this genealogical listing is explicitly stated by Matthew. The list is intentionally divided into three sections: from Abraham to David, from David to the Babylonian captivity, and from the Babylonian captivity to Christ. The list is certainly not all-inclusive, but symmetrical by purpose, fourteen generations being the item in common. It is interesting to note that Matthew has deliberately counted David in two places to give symmetry to the division. But one loses the main purpose if the ultimate object of the study is the mere recognition of the structure. The vital question is, What is the significance of this structure? Beyond any attachment of significance to the numbers three and fourteen per se, there seems to be the author's intent to recall the three great periods in the history of Israel, with the implied references to the sins of Israel and the mercy of Jehovah—accentuating the mercy and power of Jehovah in maintaining the Messi-

[13]Quoted in John Peter Lange, *Commentary on Proverbs* (Grand Rapids: Zondervan Publishing House, n.d.), p. 33.
[14]Robert D. Culver, *Daniel and the Latter Days* (Westwood, N. J.: Fleming H. Revell Co., 1954), p. 95.

anic line and giving Christ to the world. The entrance of Christ into the world from such a background is thus emphasized by the structure. Matthew gives the suggestion of the three periods; the Old Testament student fills in the details and recognizes the implications.

The second illustration is that part of the account of the flood as given in Genesis, chapters six and seven. Repetition of thought in this compositional unit is very evident. For this reason the unity of these chapters has been denied by the liberal critics. Unger says, "Of all the narratives of the Old Testament the story of the flood . . . perhaps has appeared most obviously composite to the critics."[15] It is strange indeed that the liberal critics, while claiming to do service to the field of literature by detecting different sources for the various parts of the Pentateuch, actually betray their bias by ignoring one of the basic devices of composers: repetition of thought for dramatic, didactic, and literary effect. Allis has very ably defended the unity of this deluge account by showing that the repetitions and elaborations are given to stress the three main emphases in the account, namely, the sinfulness of man as the cause of the flood, the destruction of all flesh as the aim of the flood, and the saving of a righteous remnant as the result of the flood.[16] The author of Genesis has very effectively utilized the laws of composition to give a total picture of the facts *and* their implications.

IV. LAWS OF COMPOSITION

A composition is the result of putting several thoughts together into an intended unity. The parts of the composition are made to relate to each other, as well as to the whole. John Ruskin, who has written a masterpiece entitled *Essay on Composition*, says:

[15]Unger, op. cit., p. 255.
[16]Oswald T. Allis, *The Five Books of Moses* (2d ed., Philadelphia: The Presbyterian and Reformed Publishing Co., 1949).

It is the essence of composition that everything should be in a determined place, perform an intended part, and act, in that part, advantageously for everything that is connected with it.[17]

In a composition, therefore, every part, from the least to the greatest, has its function. In a well-composed song, each note is indispensable. In a painting, each line and hue is necessary. In a writing, each word is vital. The composer's task is to create a unity (principle of principality), harmoniously arranging the various constituent parts (principle of harmony). His creation must avoid the two poles of orderly monotony and disorderly confusion. To do this, he utilizes what are called laws of composition, which are guided by the principles of harmony and principality.

A student who attempts to analyze a composition must be acquainted with the mental tools and mental processes of the composer. He must bear in mind that the composition was not created to teach or illustrate laws of composition but rather to convey a message, that message directed to the mind, emotions and the will. Therefore the student simply observes the laws of composition to determine one thing—namely, what the author wishes or intends to convey. The same aim of observation holds true in the study of a Biblical passage.

There are many laws of composition, some of which are used more frequently than others, though not necessarily more important. The following list includes most of those observed in the Biblical writings.

A. Radiation

Here the author directs the eye to one point by making various truths converge upon, or issue from, that point. Psalm 119 exemplifies this treatment, whereby God's Word

[17]Quoted in Kuist, op. cit., p. 161.

is made the principal point of reference in the experiences of the child of God.[18]

B. Repetition

Repetition is the reiteration of the *same* terms. Kuist says that if nothing is repeated in a composition, chaos rather than unity is the probable result. Repetition is perhaps the most frequently observed law in the Biblical writings. If a unit of study does not repeat the *same* terms, it will usually repeat *similar* terms. This is called by some the law of continuity. The word "see" is repeated often in John 1:35-51, while similar terms for the concept of "death" appear often in the study unit John 11:46—12:19.

C. Progression

Progression is a favorite pattern of an author in extending a theme throughout a passage, usually by addition or amplification. Many times the progression may point to an ultimate climax, though not necessarily so. In the segment Acts 5:17-42 there is a noticeable progression in the attitude of the enemies of the apostles. The sequence for the five paragraphs can be indicated by the words Jealous, Perplexed, Perturbed, Murderous, and Subdued. Oswald T. Allis, in *The Unity of Isaiah*, has shown how Isaiah, in the passage 44:24-28, has masterfully emphasized the declaration "I am the Lord" by amplifying the identification from line to line in a quantitative progression. The title which Allis gives to his diagram is: "An Arrangement of Isaiah 44:24-28 Exhibiting the Numerico-Climactic Structure of The Poem of the Transcendence of the Lord God of Israel."[19]

[18]See an interesting sequential treatment of this psalm in S. Franklin Logsdon, *Thou Art My Portion* (Grand Rapids: Zondervan Publishing House, 1956).

[19]Oswald T. Allis, *The Unity of Isaiah* (Philadelphia: The Presbyterian and Reformed Publishing Co., 1950), back insert.

D. Contrast

Contrast is the association of opposites. A poet, in employing contrast of mere structure, "purposely introduces the labouring or discordant verse, that the full ring may be felt in his main sentence, and the finished sweetness in his chosen rhythm."[20] Contrast is used effectively in all types of Biblical writing, such as the maxims of the Book of Proverbs; the logical argument of Paul in Romans; the picturesque accounts of the Gospel writers. In some instances a Gospel writer has intentionally omitted an action (such omission indicated by a comparison of the synoptic accounts), apparently to utilize the effect of contrast, by placing two contrasting elements side by side. In the Biblical writings the ranges of contrast run through all its intensities, from sharp contrast to mild comparison. A well-known contrast is the description of the two ways of Psalm 1. Within the nine verses of Acts 9:1-9 a violent contrast is portrayed in the two pictures of the persecuting Saul in his murderous march of authority and the smitten Saul in his meek submission in humility. The very frequent use of the law of contrast throughout the Bible is best explained by the fact that the major issues of the Bible involve such dual facts as good and evil, omnipotence and impotence, time and eternity, order and confusion, Heaven and Hell.

E. Climax

Climax is an extension of the law of progression. The involved progression in this case is an ascending arrangement, pointing to a peak of intensity, whether qualitative or quantitative. The classic chapter on giving, II Corinthians 9, refers climactically in the last verse to the "unspeakable gift," Jesus Christ.

[20]Kuist, op. cit., p. 176.

F. Interchange

The law of interchange, or alternation, attempts to carry at least two main thoughts in an alternating sequence, to show parallel (or contrasting) goals. An excellent example of this is found in Luke's Infancy Narrative. The alternation is: a) announcement of John's coming (1:5-25); b) announcement of Jesus' coming (1:26-56); a¹) birth of John (1:57-80); b¹) birth of Jesus (2:1-21). In this sequence both the similarities and contrasts of the stories of Jesus and John are emphasized.

G. Cruciality

The law of cruciality employs the device of the pivot. Elements on each side of the pivot differ from each other *because of* the pivot. The pivotal section in Mark's Gospel is 8:27-30, where Mark records Jesus' soliciting of answers to the question: "Who am I?" (that is, in others' estimations, and in yours). The response, "Thou art the Christ of God," becomes the pivotal phrase. The chapters preceding this section record Jesus' words and works which were spoken and performed in order to cause man to identify Jesus. Now, in the true identification given by Peter, Jesus' ministry takes a decided turn, wherein He explicitly tells His ultimate destiny and confirms that true identification of anointed deity by voluntarily walking into the way of death and resurrection.

* * *

The better acquainted the student is with the above-mentioned laws of composition, the more apt he is to recognize their utilization in a segment of study. One interesting way to become acquainted with the laws is to observe them in full-page advertisements of national magazines. Such a study will reveal, among other things, that more than one law is usually used simultaneously, a fact that holds true in Biblical composition. Ruskin's remarks are worthy of quoting in full:

> You may not readily believe, at first, that all these laws are indeed involved in so trifling a piece of composition. But, as you study longer, you will discover that these laws, and many more, are obeyed by the powerful composers in every *touch:* that literally, there is never a dash of their pencil which is not carrying out appointed purposes of this kind in twenty various ways at once; and that there is as much difference, in way of intention and authority, between one of the great composers ruling his colours, and a common painter confused by them, as there is between a general directing the march of an army, and an old lady carried off her feet by a mob.[21]

The Bible student cannot hope to know fully all of the thought processes of the Biblical authors as they were moved to compose God's message, for the simple reason that their unique experience of inspiration has been neither described in detail nor shared experientially by other men. This fact, however, should not discourage any phase of intensive Bible study, but rather challenge it. Any discipline of study, including the observation of the form of a composition, should be welcomed by the Bible student in his quest to really know *what God wrote.* If being aware of compositional laws in the text of the Bible opens new and fresh avenues of vista for the student, then such study is fully justified.

---

[21]Quoted in Kuist, op. cit., p. 176.

Chapter II

THE INDUCTIVE METHOD OF STUDY

IN THIS DAY of synthetics, speed, compactness, and brevity, the atmosphere for solid, thorough, independent methodical Bible study is almost prohibitive. For meditations, a few verses are read. In study, the student exposes himself unpurposefully to the content of a set of detached verses, fleeing to the refuge of worthy commentaries and aids to the point where he masters the aids and does not know the Bible. In the pulpit, the preacher either speaks a verse-by-verse commentary, or confines himself almost exclusively to topical messages, delivering expository messages only occasionally. More than half a century ago the same weaknesses of Bible study and communication challenged Wilbert W. White, founder of The Biblical Seminary in New York, to take a method of study and adapt it to the Holy Scriptures—a method known, and still commonly known, as the inductive method. In teaching this method to others it was Dr. White's aim primarily to develop independent and original students of the Bible.

I. DESCRIPTION OF THE METHOD

The essential facts of the inductive method are aptly illustrated by the well-known experience of the student, seeking to learn something in a special area of zoology, who approached his professor, J. Louis Agassiz of Harvard University. (See Appendix II for the complete story.) Given a pickled specimen of a fish, a haemulon, which was to be the sole object of his scrutiny, the student learned over a period of three long days what was involved in gaining a thorough knowledge of the fish. The advice of the professor was to the point. (1) The student was to "look, look, look!", for how else could he master the subject? (2) He was to draw on paper what he saw, for "the pencil is one of the best eyes." (3) He was to recognize the parts of the haemulon in their orderly arrangement and relations to each other, for "facts are stupid things until brought into connection with some general law." That this method of study was fruitful to the point of live absorption is indicated by the student's later testimony: "To this day, if I attempt [to draw] a fish, I can draw nothing but haemulons."

Andrew W. Blackwood has recognized the necessity of this absorbing process in one's Bible study in preparation for the ministry of preaching. He writes:

> Before a man dares to preach much about the Christ of the Fourth Gospel, he ought to live with this book for a number of months. In case of difficulty he should consult a first-class exegetical commentary. . . . But the main stress ought to fall on reading the Bible book itself, as it was written, and on dealing with each paragraph as a unit.[1]

A. The Inductive Method Is Scientific in Approach

The inductive method of Bible study is scientific in its order of procedure: (1) It begins with the observable—what do you see here? (2) It follows with the interpretative—what does it mean? (3) It pleads for application—how does this affect you? In observing a passage of Scripture, the student is urged to lay the passage before him in temporary isolation, and to approach it impartially and fearlessly. He should scrutinize it with what John Ruskin calls "the innocence of the eye"—as if he had never seen it before. As he weighs each part, there should be calmness, deliberateness, and extreme care in his movements. He breathes the air of

[1]Andrew W. Blackwood, "Giving Christ the Place of Honor," *Christianity Today*, IV, 8 (January 18, 1960), p. 7.

expectancy, and cherishes his eye as an honest servant of the mind. What he desires above all else, in a true scientific approach, is to see things *as they really are*.

Strictly speaking, induction and deduction are opposite methods. In induction, one first observes, then concludes. In deduction one begins with a general principle or conclusion, then observes whether the conclusion is true. Stated another way, "Induction is the logic of discovery, while deduction is the logic of proof."[2] Francis Bacon likened the deductive method to the spider spinning its web out of itself, while he compared induction to the bee's intense engagement in flights from flower to flower to gather its store of honey. In practice, one cannot use pure induction exclusively without cutting short a full Bible study, for the two processes of induction and deduction are mutually dependent. A Christian cannot begin a study of a Bible passage in a vacuum. For efficient progress in study, deduction should supplement induction at every point.

B. The Inductive Method Is Analytical in Character

When the student is face to face with the minute parts of Scripture, including even the punctuation, and when he wrestles to know its intent in its context, he is engaging in the study process known as analysis. Analysis is distinguished by its exactness, minuteness, and comprehensiveness. Merrill C. Tenney makes a high appraisal of the analytical method when he says, "In order to ascertain exactly what a given body of text says, one should employ the analytical method."[3]

The student analyzes the Bible itself, not words about the Bible. The tendency for the average Bible student at the outset of a study is to rally all types of aids that will do the seeing and thinking for him. Such a flight to aids usually

[2]Charles Eberhardt, *The Bible in the Making of Ministers* (New York: Association Press, 1949), p. 130.
[3]Merrill C. Tenney, *The Genius of the Gospels*, p. 165.

arises out of a sense of inadequacy on the student's part. C. S. Lewis found this same tendency among his students of English literature at Cambridge University of England. He observed that if the average student wanted to study Plato, the very last thing he thought of doing was to take a translation of Plato and read *Plato*. Instead, he would read long books *about Plato*. If the student only knew, said Lewis, that Plato is much more intelligible than his modern commentator!

Analysis involves structure, for structure, as described in the previous chapter, involves two things: parts, and the relations of parts to each other and to the whole. Words, phrases, and sentences constitute the unit of thought called a *paragraph;* a group of paragraphs constitutes a unit, averaging approximately twenty to twenty-five verses in the Bible, which may be arbitrarily called a *segment.* The Bible student, then, in analyzing a segment recognizes that, since the segment is a unit of thought, it has one primary truth which the author has imparted, and, since the paragraphs within the segment are units of thought, they also can each be identified with a distinct unifying truth, which in turn relates to the grand thought of the segment. The implications of such a structure are tremendous. For instance, the second paragraph of a segment may *appear* to have no necessary relation to the first or third paragraph, and yet the student knows it is where it is for a purpose and in line with a plan, and he is challenged to find that purpose. Many thrilling nuggets of gold have been discovered from such a study of relationships, wherein one recognizes, as White often said, that "things hook and eye together." Of course, the same structure-consciousness applies to the analysis of words, phrases, and sentences within a paragraph.

C. The Inductive Method Is Re-creative in Purpose

Re-creative study does not imply that the Bible needs to

be rewritten, or improved upon. Rather, it seeks to bring into being in the mind of the reader a clear grasp of the writer's message. It is a study discipline involving three things:

1. rediscovery of what the authors—human and divine—intended to *say;*
2. recognition of what the authors *meant;*
3. receptivity to the divine message by a submissive and obedient spirit. ·

The re-creative discipline respects the supernatural co-existence of diversity and unity in the sixty-six books of the Bible. All of its conclusions must conform to the grand truths revealed throughout Scripture regarding God and His creation. All Scripture is viewed in the light of the Christological key to the Bible's unity.

The diversity of content may be associated in the Bible with that which is in a given *local* situation, while the unity of content may be associated with that which is *universal.* For instance, one recognizes throughout the Scriptures the doctrine of the sinfulness of sin—sin for which there is eternal judgment because it is violation of the law of the eternal God. This truth about sin is universally applicable—at all times and in all places—and so it is not surprising that all the Scriptures teach the same truth. The story of Ananias and Sapphira, in addition to teaching a universal truth, has a local content in its relating the judgment for a lie, such judgment being the immediate smiting to death of the instigators of the lie. The Bible student distinguishes between that which is locally applicable and that which is universally applicable, and concludes that (1) all liars are not struck dead on the spot for lying, though this was the way of God on this specific occasion, and (2) the universal dictum is reiterated: "Whatsoever a man soweth, that shall he also reap."

In his task of re-creating the Biblical text, the Bible student must be able to distinguish between the local and the universal. St. Augustine said, "Distinguish the times and you harmonize the Scriptures." The Bible student furthermore must sit at the desk of the Biblical author and converse with him as his pen delivers its eternal message. In empathy he must weep with the prophet, rejoice with the psalmist, and exhort with the apostle. And if he can so transport himself to the chamber where the holy men of God wrote being moved by the Holy Spirit, the written Word will become a living and transforming power in his own daily life, to the glory of God.

II. AIMS AND PROCEDURES OF THE INDUCTIVE METHOD

A. What Does the Author Intend to Say?

1. *Emphasis of a principal truth*

Because of the complexity of structure of much of the Biblical writings, Bible study is easily bogged down if the detailed side paths are traversed prematurely. The writer of a book of the Bible did not record a host of unrelated words in endless babblings, but composed the writing with one basic overall intent, the various parts of the book harmoniously reflecting the same underlying principle of principality. If the Bible student is to discover those principal truths, he must be aware of the methods used by the author, consciously or otherwise, in emphasizing such truths.

The question may be asked whether a Bible student who has not been trained in the Hebrew and Greek languages, in which most of the Old and New testaments were originally written, can adequately capture the author's intents from the English translation of his writings. The enriching value of a working knowledge of the original languages should not be underestimated. However, our various good English versions, especially when studied in comparison one with the other, faithfully reproduce the impact of most of the crucial words and phrases of the Bible. This is no coincidence, for the editorial committees of such English versions usually represent an impressive background of scholarship in the original languages. All versions of the Bible in the vernacular tongues have this common purpose of translating, as faithfully as possible, the original languages into the mother tongue, so as to guarantee what is most evidently God's will —that the Bible be for the laity as well as for the professionally trained scholar.

In this connection it may be pointed out that a keen sense of controlled imagination is a very practical aid in determining the force of an English word as it was intended in the original language. For example, Matthew 9:36 describes Jesus as being moved with compassion for the multitudes, because they were "distressed and scattered, as sheep not having a shepherd." If one will imagine the many dangers which can befall sheep which are shepherdless, he will perceive the intensity and the awful implications involved in the words "distressed" and "scattered," which are borne out by their original words, meaning, respectively, "plagued" and "beaten down prostrate."

The further outside help in Greek and Hebrew which the Bible student is encouraged to use, beyond his independent study, will be referred to later on in connection with auxiliary aids. It may be observed at this point that such help involves mainly word studies and grammatical relations. When it comes to the broader structural studies, involving the relation of paragraph to paragraph and segment to segment, the student is most efficient in the version of his mother tongue. Hence the inductive method of study is utilized very effectively in the study of the *English* Bible.

a. Identification of structural variety

In the study of a passage of the Bible it is obvious that

some of the communication is primary, while other parts are subordinate; also, some elements are obvious, while others are more elusive as to detection. The student should be aware of this diversity in the structure of the passage, for the purposes of the author are involved.

(1) As to importance: the primary and the subordinate

It is not always easy to identify that which is primary in the structure of a writing. In any case, it is vital that the student arrive at such an identification as early as possible in his methodical study. Many misleading interpretations have been made because that which was intended to be subordinate has been identified wrongly as primary. A jot never constituted a full word, nor a tittle, a whole letter. A sound hermeneutical maxim for the interpretation of parables, for example, is that a parable is intended to teach one primary truth and, in some cases, may teach additional subordinate truths. It is the student's task to identify what is primary and what, if anything, is intended to teach a subordinate lesson.

(2) As to apparency: the obvious and the latent

In any given passage there may be found that which is evident, unequivocal, and explicit and, on the other hand, that which is hidden, elusive, and implicit. The differences do not necessarily indicate differences in importance or depth of spiritual significance. Actually, such differences can be accounted for in various ways. From the author's standpoint, the utilization of the less apparent may involve the emphasis of a primary truth by way of contrast, or any of the various compositional laws and grammatical relations may be involved. From the student's standpoint, the less apparent may be a relative classification, depending on the student's natural abilities of observation and perception, or depending on his spiritual acumen. What must not be lost sight of is that the purpose of the inductive method of study is to ascertain *what the Scriptures themselves were intended to say*, as the authors were inspired by the Holy Spirit.

b. Methods used by the author (structural makeup)

(1) Atmosphere

The atmosphere of a segment of study in the Bible will sometimes give a clue as to why the writer chose a certain sequence in the account. In each of the paragraphs throughout the segment might lie a pervading atmosphere of hate, or expectancy, or peace, or doubt. This tone device of atmosphere is intended to help the student "feel" the impact of the sum of the words, and in this total approach he begins to see something of the overall purposes of the writer.

(2) Relative quantity

The quantitative clue to emphases is detected when space devoted to one subject is intentionally made long or short as compared to what is devoted to other subjects in the unit of study. This is not to be construed as meaning that the shorter the discussion of a subject is, the less important it is, and vice versa. Actually, the author may have chosen to emphasize a truth by using few words to tell it. How else can one interpret the intent of John 11:35: "Jesus wept"? An example of large quantity with reference to time is found in John's Gospel where the first eleven and one-half chapters relate to three years of Jesus' earthly ministry, while the remaining nine and one-half chapters relate to only a few days. Or, consider the following distribution of space in Luke's Gospel to the various periods in Jesus' life:

PREPARATION	PROCLAMATION	P A S S I O N	
1	4:14	9:18	19:28 24
		TO JERUSALEM	AT JERUSALEM

This pattern in the Gospels clearly emphasizes the supreme importance of the death and resurrection of Christ as compared to the events leading up to those crises.

However, the quantitative clue does not always have a temporal element involved. For example, the relatively large space devoted to a listing of the works of the flesh and the fruit of the Spirit in the paragraph of Galatians 5:16-24 is a clue to the principal teaching in that paragraph. This is what may be called topical relative quantity.

(3) Grammatical structure

The usual order of words in a simple declarative sentence is: subject, verb, object. Many times this "core" is lost to the student in an extended sentence involving many modifying clauses. For example, if one looks at the long sentence of Hebrews 1:1-4, he will recognize a very complex statement woven into the following core (capital letters indicating the core):[4]

GOD,   having of old time spoken
                unto the fathers
                in the prophets
                by divers portions and in divers manners,
HATH   at the end of these days
SPOKEN   unto us
                IN A SON,
                    whom he appointed heir of all things,
                    through whom also he made the worlds;
                    WHO
                        being the effulgence of his glory,
                        and the very image of his substance,
                        and upholding all things by the word of his
                            power, when he had made purification of sins,
                    SAT DOWN
                        on the right hand of the Majesty on high;

[4]Text is from the American Standard Version. Actually, this grammatical structure involves two cores.

having become, by so much, better than the
angels,
as he hath inherited a more excellent name than
they.

(A.S.V.)

It is evident that this core, *"God hath spoken* in a *Son who sat down,"* reflects the principal truth which the author intends to convey. A closer analysis of the structure of the four verses reveals the following comparison:

"God"

"having spoken"	"hath spoken"
"unto the fathers"	"unto us"
"in the prophets"	"in a Son"
"by divers portions and in divers manners"	"WHO SAT DOWN"
(Progressive, Continuous Revelation)	(Completed Revelation)

From this vantage point of analysis, the phrase "who sat down" is seen to be the principal phrase within the principal core, emphasizing the vital truth that revelation has found its completion in the person and work of Christ.

In both Hebrew and Greek a study of the syntax of the sentences often reveals the importance or significance of a word or phrase as is demanded by its relative position in the word order of the sentence. For example, the phrase of Ephesians 3:16b reads in the following order in the English version: "that ye may be strengthened with power through his Spirit in the inward man." In the Greek text the order of words runs thus: *"with power* to be strengthened by his Spirit in the inner man." The word for "power" appears first, apparently for emphasis. Frequently the order of the Greek or Hebrew is not carried over into the English versions, and such clues are therefore not forthcoming in the study of the English text.

(4) Laws of composition

Since a composer utilizes compositional laws in guaranteeing harmony and principality in his work, it is obvious that the recognition of these laws by the student leads to the discerning of those intended principal ideas. Since units of study usually betray more than one compositional law, the concurrence of observed "data" in this area of study must be sought if the principal ideas are to be identified.

(5) The unexpected or unnatural

Someone has said, "An observer will have his eyes open to notice anything which according to received theories ought not to happen, for these are the facts which serve as clues to new discoveries."[5] Liberal higher criticism usually accounts for the unexpected element as being misplaced, injected into the writing from another author or by a scribe, or incomplete. The Bible student who accepts the present text as substantially pure and faithful to the originals, is not satisfied with that solution, however. He recognizes that all the parts of the composition, whether "unnatural" or not, are where they are for a reason. He rightly recognizes that all authors of compositions utilize purposeful selectivity in what is included in *and* excluded from the writing. If this is true for human authorship, how much more is it not true for divine-human authorship?

Therefore it may be said also that what seems to be an omission has its purpose. Stevenson is quoted as saying, "To omit . . . is the one art of literature."[6] The rather abrupt ending of the Acts of the Apostles, when viewed as with purpose, suggests, among other things, that God caused the

---

[5]Quoted in Robert Traina, *Methodical Bible Study* (privately published, 1952), p. 75.
[6]Ibid.

book to be written before other events had occurred, including Paul's death, to emphasize the *continuing* work of the *Holy Spirit*, beyond the decease of any human servant, and thus to direct the reader's eyes to the *continuing* story as contained in the epistles and in the forthcoming history of the Church.

    c. Contexts where the principal lines of thought are observed (structural contexts)

    (1) Entire book, and large divisions

In the "skyscraper" view of the entire book, the primary task of the student is to observe the *main* trend of thought. General impressions are gathered in this cursory reading as the student recognizes atmosphere or mood, relative emphasis placed upon a subject, obvious compositional laws such as repetition and contrast, ideological train of thought, and anything of the unexpected (e.g. things that strike one for the first time). Since most Biblical writers have not explicitly stated the major purpose of their writings, as John has for his Gospel (John 20:30-31), it is the Bible student's task to evaluate the above-mentioned general observations and impressions in order to understand the author's main purpose.

As with any compositional unit, there are, through the pattern of a Bible book, subordinate or auxiliary developments of subjects in addition to that which is primary. For example, in the three major divisions of Acts (1:1-8:1a; 8:1b-12:25; 13:1–28:31) may be seen various developments, such as:

    (*a*) geographical: Jerusalem, Judea and Samaria, ends of the earth
    (*b*) biographical: Peter, Peter and Paul, Paul
    (*c*) historical: Jewish Period, Transitional Period, Gentile Period

The *overall* purpose of Luke in writing Acts appears to be a factual account of the early church's Spirit-empowered witness to Christ. It should be noted, however, that any auxiliary structure, like the three outlines given above, is not to be considered as unimportant. Actually, the *parts* of any structure, by virtue of their very use, are indispensable in giving the distinctiveness to that structure.

Many times the overall purpose of a book is derived by observing the main intent of each of the *large divisions* within that book. The same observational procedures apply to divisional study as apply to book study.

(2) Segment and paragraphs

If a segment, which is approximately the length of an average chapter, is a compositional unity of study, it follows that it is intended to communicate one central truth. Likewise each of its paragraphs has one unifying thought, all of which relate to the segment's central truth. The student, therefore, attempts to identify these major themes as early as possible in his study procedure, in order that he may adequately recognize the service of the many details within the segment.

Just as auxiliary outlines are detected in the main structure of an entire book of the Bible, so auxiliary themes and topical studies are developed within a segment. And seemingly endless numbers of studies are brought into focus depending on the "window" or vantage point within the text from which the analysis is made.

(3) The sentence

In the many grammatically complex sentences of the Bible it is mandatory that the student recognize the "core" of such sentences, which, as stated previously, usually involves the main subject, verb, and object. The sentences of the Old Testament are not usually complex, for the reason that the Hebrew writer expresses himself in a concrete, forthright, and direct manner. Someone has observed, for example, that there is no indirect speech in the Hebrew Old Testament.[7] In the New Testament, on the other hand, especially in the epistles, many sentences are the length of more than one verse, involving all types of subordinate clauses. The core of the following long sentence in Romans 2:17-23 is found toward the end of the sentence (indicated by the italicized phrases):

But if thou bearest the name of a Jew,
and restest upon the law,
and gloriest in God,
and knowest his will,
and approvest the things that are excellent,
being instructed out of the law,
and art confident that thou thyself art a guide of the blind,
   a light of them that are in darkness,
   a corrector of the foolish,
   a teacher of babes,
having in the law the form of knowledge and of the truth;
thou therefore that teachest another, *teachest thou not*
                                    thyself?
thou that preachest a man should not steal, *dost thou steal?*
thou that sayest a man should not commit adultery, *dost*
                            thou commit adultery?
thou that abhorrest idols, *dost thou rob temples?*
thou who gloriest in the law, through thy transgression of
          the law *dishonorest thou God?*

(Romans 2:17-23, A.S.V.)

There is another type of sentence in which something other than the main subject, verb, and object forms the core.

[7]F. F. Bruce, *The Books and the Parchments* (3d ed.; Westwood, N. J.: Fleming H. Revell Co., 1963), p. 45.

For example, the entire paragraph of Ephesians 1:3-14 is one long sentence,[8] compacted with scores of deep truths of Christian faith and living. The main subject and verb appear in the opening words,

"Blessed (be) (the) God and Father,"

or, "God and Father" "be blessed."

However, this phrase is not the key to the principal thought of the sentence. The interpenetration of the long sentence by such words and phrases as "in him," "before him," and "in Christ," really determines the core. The diagram of this sentence given below shows this core in the middle column. The phrases in the left-hand column have reference, generally, to the past, while those in the right-hand column have reference, generally, to the present and future.

Blessed be the God and Father of
our Lord Jesus Christ, who hath blessed us
with every spiritual blessing in the heavenly places

PAST   PRESENT AND FUTURE

IN CHRIST:

even as he chose us   IN HIM
before the foundation of
the world,
                                 that we should be holy and
                                 without blemish
                         BEFORE HIM   in love:

having foreordained us
unto adoption as sons   THROUGH JESUS CHRIST unto himself,
according to the good
pleasure of his will, to
the praise of the glory
of his grace, which he
freely bestowed on us   IN THE BELOVED:

                         IN WHOM   we have our redemption
                         THROUGH HIS BLOOD, the forgiveness of our
                                      trespasses,

[8]American Standard Version. B. F. Westcott, who refers to this passage as a psalm of praise, recognizes a rhythmical structure in the verses. Referring to this, he says, "The rhythmical structure of the passage will be apparent, if it is arranged according to the succession of the principal clauses; and at the same time some obscurities of construction will be removed when attention is fixed on the dominant finite verbs." *St. Paul's Epistle to the Ephesians* (Grand Rapids: Wm. B. Eerdmans Publishing Co., 1950), p. 5.

according to the riches of
his grace, which he made to
abound toward us in all wisdom and prudence, making
known unto us the mystery of
his will, according to his good
pleasure which he purposed IN HIM   unto a dispensation of the
fulness of the times,
to sum up all things
    IN CHRIST, the things in the heavens,
and the things upon the earth,
    IN HIM,   I say,
    IN WHOM
also we were made a heritage,
having been foreordained ac-
cording to the purpose of him who   worketh all things after
the counsel of his will;
to the end that we should
be unto the praise of his
glory,

we who had before hoped   IN CHRIST:
    IN WHOM
ye also, having heard the
word of the truth, the
gospel of your salvation,—   IN WHOM,
having also believed, ye
were sealed with the Holy
Spirit of promise,   which is an earnest of our
inheritance, unto the
redemption of God's own
possession, unto the praise
of his glory.

Ephesians 1:3-14, A.S.V.

A similar example of this type of core is found in the very next paragraph of Ephesians 1 where, again, the entire paragraph (vv. 15-23) is all one sentence. In this sentence the main subject and verb is found in the phrase "I ... cease not (to give thanks)"; but again, this is not the clue to that which is primary. Rather, the phrase *that ye may know* (v. 18) becomes the key, or core phrase.

* * *

It is very evident, therefore, that from the smallest complete structural unit (sentence) to the longest (book), the author's principal lines of thought are woven therein, and therefore to be detected by the student.

2. *Message to a real situation*

The universal applicability of the Bible to the human race has its first demonstration in the fact that God's Word, as it was transmitted through the instrumentality of the various human authors, was usually directed to a real situation. While the Bible continually refers to the other world, it is certainly not ethereal, dreamy, or visionary. It does not portray fanciful escapades of men's minds into unreality, but always treads the path of stark reality.

a. Varieties of situations contemporaneous with the author

The individual historical books of the Old Testament came into the hands of their first readers to meet the contemporary need of written revelation, teaching such vital truths as those about man, sin, God, and the heritage of covenant-hope. The prophets themselves, while foretelling very distant events, at the same time were forthtelling and foretelling a message of *immediate* application for their contemporaries. The apocalypse of John, so much of which had to do with "things hereafter," was written to encourage and instruct Christians who at the close of the first century were undergoing severe persecution.

It is necessary therefore, if a student wishes to re-create or understand the Biblical author's full intentions, that he come to grips with the immediate or contemporary situation for or about which the author originally wrote.

(1) Need for factual information

Since God is the Creator and Ruler of the universe, history

in the broad sense is the sequence of all events, recorded or unrecorded, *in relation to God.* In a very real sense, any history book which accurately records historical facts involving individuals and groups of individuals (race, nation, alliance, etc.) contributes to a knowledge of God, disclosing such things as His permissive will or efficient will. One of the greatest modern historians, Arnold J. Toynbee, defines history as "a vision—dim and partial, yet . . . true to reality as far as it went—of God revealing Himself in action to souls that were sincerely seeking Him."[9]

If so-called "secular" history books contribute to a knowledge of God, how much more should the Biblical historical books have to offer in this respect! Surely such books as Genesis were written to describe, even *for the generations of their first reading,* the ways of man (basically sinful) and the ways of God (holy, just, gracious, long-suffering, etc.). Of course, even in the so-called historical books there are those sections which were intended to do more than give description or example, such as the recording of the Decalogue (Exodus 20) and Levitical laws (Leviticus) to be incorporated in the very worship of the people of God.

Since so much of the Bible is factual in nature, involving, in addition to history, such areas of knowledge as geography, culture, psychology, and nature, it is vital that the Bible student have access to extra-Biblical sources for further light on such subjects. There are numerous up-to-date Bible dictionaries, encyclopedias, atlases, geographies, and archaeological works which make rich contributions to an understanding of the ancient situations to which and about which the Biblical authors wrote.

(2) Need for correction and warning

All Scripture is profitable for reproof and correction

[9]Arnold J. Toynbee, *A Study of History,* Vol. X (London: Oxford University Press, 1954), p. 1.

(II Tim. 3:16). It cannot be said, however, that the intent of the Holy Spirit in the local setting of every book of the Bible was always primarily corrective. For example, the primary intention of the Book of Acts was not corrective but instructive (Acts 1:1-2). On the other hand, there are many parts of Scripture that were intended primarily to correct the addressee. This is true of many of the ringing messages of the prophets of the Old Testament and of the writers of the New Testament epistles. Much of I Corinthians was written to correct existing conditions in the local church at Corinth.

In the interpretive process of Bible study great care must be exercised in distinguishing between the basic principle and the local detail at which the reproof is aimed. Here again, especially in the epistles, an acquaintance with the cultural backgrounds of the Biblical setting can be a crucial element in the interpretive exercise of the Bible student.

(3) Need for encouragement and stimulation

The Old Testament fathers and prophets, as well as the New Testament writers, supplemented their negative approach of reproof with the warm appeals of encouragement and stimulation. One senses an antiphonal effect as the two approaches—reproof and inspiration—are often alternately used, almost in the same breath. The Psalms are infused with soul-stirring messages, and an appreciation of the Revelation of John is enhanced when one recognizes that, among other purposes, it was intended to encourage and give hope to disappointed and bewildered Christians undergoing the hardships of persecution.

(4) Need for doctrine

Doctrine, or formal teaching, is the primary intent of much of the epistolary writing of the New Testament. Since the New Testament is the embodiment and culmination of the foundational truths of the Old Testament revelation, one would expect to see such a concentration of doctrine here. The student must recognize, however, that the Biblical author did not intend to set forth a systematized or comprehensive order of doctrine and, therefore, erroneous interpretations by way of implication must be avoided.

It is axiomatic that the Biblical author should not be made to say more than he has said. Cross-reference study, or the citing of verses from other parts of the Bible which teach truths associated with that of the verse under scrutiny, is a profitable exercise in one's study procedure, especially in word studies. This process of using Scripture to interpret Scripture has been one of the soundest maxims in exegesis. But for segment studies, it is best first to concentrate one's study on the words and thoughts in their immediate context and use cross-reference study later as a supplementary guide. This is sound procedure in the inductive method of study because:

(a) *It respects the author's selectivity.* The segment of study contains that which the Holy Spirit deemed sufficient in its context.

(b) *It preserves innocence of the eye.* The student's immediate task is to see *what the segment says for itself.* The nurturing of multitudinous related studies in the middle of such an objective activity of mind may easily give rise to many tangents of thought which lead nowhere.

(c) *It demands an exhaustive analysis of parts and their relations to each other.* For example, if an ambiguous word or phrase occurs in a segment of study, the student will not be satisfied until the context sheds some light on its meaning.

   b. Real situations through the centuries

When Paul reviewed for the Corinthian church many of the experiences of the Israelites of Old Testament days, he said, "Now these things happened unto them by way of example; and they were written for our admonition, upon whom the ends of the ages are come" (I Cor. 10:11, A.S.V.). If the Scriptural history of the two millennia previous to Paul's epistle was profitably applicable to his day, this is sufficient demonstration of the enduring applicability of the Bible throughout all centuries. Of all books, the Bible stands alone, not only as uniquely universal, but universally timeless.

This is not to say, of course, that the customs and cultures of believers in Old Testament days are the same as those of believers in the present century. The Bible student must identify the local temporal detail, and relate it to the universal timeless principle, if he is to find a present-day application. On the other hand, the weightier factors of human experience and behavior are not seen to change significantly through the centuries for the reason that human nature does not change. Disobedience and pride in the Garden of Eden are the disobedience and pride of today. The soul experiences of Paul the Apostle are the soul experiences of a modern apostle of the same spiritual stature.

It is not difficult for the consecrated Christian Bible student to sense that the Bible is speaking to real situations in the present century. As he studies the Scriptures he sees himself portrayed with all his flaws, weaknesses, and shortcomings, as well as with his hopes and desires. He sees God as the unchanging Eternal One, whose ways with men do not vary. He sees the eternal law of returns—"Whatsoever a man soweth that shall he also reap"—as effective today as it was thousands of years ago.

In a particular Bible passage with reference to a particular situation in life, then, the Bible student identifies whether the situation is of local and temporal application or of universal and timeless application. In the case of the former, the student further seeks to identify the universal and timeless *principle* involved in the local. *All* of the Scriptures, therefore, are seen to be continually applicable for all time—and eternity.

c. Varieties of literary media
(1) Kinds of terms

Strong and routine. Since the Bible is literature, the authors have written the eternal truths in sentence form. It is obvious that within one given sentence there are words which are weighty or strong while all others within the same sentence are weaker or routine. Many words of the latter classification serve in the text only to form a complete sentence. When Mark refers to Jesus' reply to Pilate's question, "Art thou the King of the Jews?", he records thus (Mark 15:2b):

> And he answering saith unto him, Thou sayest.

In the context it is obvious that the words, "And he answering saith unto him," are of the routine classification, especially since they serve only in a formal sense to connect the narrative. The words, "Thou sayest," are strong words, not only because of their factual content but also because of their pungent quality.

Care should be exercised in not forcing hermeneutical importance to the routine or accidental in a sentence. This has been an error of some exegetes as far back as the rabbinical interpreters. Distinguishing the strong from the routine terms can be difficult or easy, depending on the sentence and the context. In either case, making the distinctions is an important procedure in one's ascertainment of the author's intent.

Literal and figurative. Figures of speech, comprising figurative words and figures of thought, e.g., simile and metaphor, are found throughout the Bible. However, most of the Bible uses literal rather than figurative language. In interpretation, the literal approach, which is also the normal approach to all literature, recognizes both kinds of usage, and interprets accordingly.

Much of the figurative language of the Bible is intended to throw light on that which is *spiritual*, since in human language there is no substantial "heavenly" vocabulary to describe the spiritual world. Some examples of such spiritual truths, with figurative language used to describe them, are:

God's nature and works—	"Jehovah my *fortress*" "The Lord is my *shepherd*"
Relation between Christ and believers—	"I am the *vine*, ye are the *branches*"
Aspects of salvation—	"*redeem*" "*born* again"
Kinds of sins—	"*puffed up*" "having *itching ears*"
Soul experiences of man—	"I am a *worm*"

The images borrowed from daily life afford impressive and accurate revelation concerning these otherwise "hidden" truths. Their accuracy is no doubt attributed in part to the divine harmony between the natural and spiritual worlds.

Since such important spiritual truths are conveyed by figurative language, it is essential that the Bible student become proficient in the interpretation of such language. His task is twofold: (1) to ascertain what is figurative in a passage, and (2) to determine the truth intended by the original author through that figure—no more and no less. In most passages, the student should have no serious difficulty with either task. (The Book of Revelation is a notable exception.)

For the first task, he should follow the sound interpretative principle that words should be interpreted literally unless this leads to contradiction or absurdity. Common-sense judgment is necessary here.

For the second task, that of determining what spiritual truth is being taught by the figure of speech, the student needs to identify the picture for which the *context* is calling. For example, the word "shepherd" could in a certain context emphasize the *lowly* aspect of such a man's occupation. However, for the phrase, "The Lord is my shepherd," the context of the twenty-third Psalm indicates that the *guidance, protection* and *provision* aspects of shepherding are being taught.

Common sense and context, then, are the two key helpmates in identifying the Biblical author's intentions in his use of literal and figurative language.

(2) Kinds of literature

Each of the authors of the Bible, inspired by the Holy Spirit, composed the divine message in a form of literature that represented one of the ways of writing in his day. The forms of ancient literature—prose, poetry, etc.—have not perished, but remain as the forms also of modern literature. When one considers that the Bible was written by more than thirty-five authors with diverse backgrounds, it is not surprising to see such a variety of literary forms represented in the Scriptures.

In seeking to understand what the Biblical author intended to say, it is necessary, among other things, that the student recognize the outer literary form. Richard Moulton contends that just as interpreting Scripture with faulty ideas of its grammar and syntax would be running the risk of "fundamental errors in theological or historical inferences," even so a risk is involved in drawing theological or historical interpretations from a Scripture whose literary structure is ignored.[10]

It is indeed unfortunate that the existence of such a variety of literary forms in Scripture has been obscured by the way in which the Bible has been printed in most versions. Moulton, who contends that "the Bible has come down to us as the worst-printed book in the world," refers to its format as a "succession of numbered sentences, with divisions into longer or shorter chapters, under which all trace of dramatic, lyric, story, essay, is hopelessly lost."[11] One of the values of a few of the modern versions for the Bible student is that much of the literary form has been retained in the format, e.g., poetry, even in a prophetic book, is printed in stanza form.

In the previous chapter reference was made to the two basic kinds of writing, namely, prose and poetry. Under the former classification may be listed history, philosophy (or reflection), and rhetoric. Epic, lyric, and drama may be classified as types of poetry. The error of not detecting drama in the Book of Job can be disastrous, for, as Moulton points out, the student may take the words of one of the actors, like Bildad the Shuhite, as being true, whereas God in the final chapter identifies his words as untrue. The sudden change of tone between verses six and seven in Micah 7 caused the higher critic Wellhausen incorrectly to conclude that between those verses "yawns a century." Actually, as Moulton observes, the section 6:9—7:20 gives a sequence of dramatic speeches by different speakers, and the words of 7:7 are a different voice from that of 7:6.

Three types of Biblical writing within the above-men-

---

[10]Richard G. Moulton, *A Short Introduction to the Literature of the Bible* (Boston: D. C. Heath and Co., Publishers, 1909), p. 6.
[11]Ibid., p. 9.

tioned literary classifications, in addition to prose and poetry, may be cited here.

Wisdom literature. Job, Proverbs, Ecclesiastes, and the Song of Solomon were written in the style of wisdom literature, where the authors are seen observing life and the world. The word "observation" is a key word in indicating the tone of wisdom literature. This tone differs from that of poetry, where worship is predominant; or of prophecy, where authority is stressed; or of the Law, where revelation and guidance are the keynotes. Moulton interestingly distinguishes the content of the wisdom literature of the Bible by stages, thus:

1. Proverbs: stage of philosophic calm
2. Ecclesiastes: stage of storm and stress
3. Song of Solomon: later stage of triumph
4. Book of Job: (wisdom dramatized)

Parabolic literature. Parables, which are found in both testaments and are to be distinguished from myth, allegory, fable, or proverb, are intended by the Biblical speakers or writers to teach spiritual truths. The originator of a parable, such as Jesus, in the course of a teaching discourse describes a common earthly event, sight, custom, or thing without usually giving the intended interpretation thereof. On some occasions Jesus gave the interpretation of the parable. Exegetes have always differed as to whether a parable is intended to teach one main truth or whether *many* of the details are to be spiritualized as well. Because Jesus spiritualized various details of a parable on more than one occasion, the Bible student must recognize at least the possibility of similar intentions for other parables. Whatever arguments are advanced for both sides of this hermeneutical problem, however, it is the feeling of the present writer that the student is on firm ground by taking the central truth as the leading and most important truth, and letting it guide one's inquiry into any bordering cognate truths. Richard C.

Trench's advice on determining how much of the parable is to be spiritualized is recorded in his classic work, *Notes on the Parables of Our Lord*, thus:

> Much must be left to good sense, to spiritual tact, to that reverence for the word of God, which will show itself sometimes in refusing curiosities of interpretation, no less than at other times in demanding a distinct spiritual meaning for the words which are before it.[12]

When the student has determined, at least for the time being, how much of the parable was intended for spiritualization, the next crucial step is arriving at the interpretations themselves. Among the various maxims for interpreting parables, the rule of surrounding context offers the student the most light for his interpretation. Any context which answers the following two questions is gold to the interpreter:

1. What brought on the parable?
2. What effect did the parable have on the hearers?

Because parables speak of daily life, an understanding of the items in the parable relating to custom, culture, geography, etc. of the Biblical days is also essential to a full appreciation of the intent of the parable.

There are various hermeneutical helps for the student in his quest for the interpretations of parables. Two of the best works devoted to the subject are Archbishop Trench's work, referred to above, and G. Campbell Morgan's *The Parables and Metaphors of Our Lord*. The student is urged, however, always to keep in mind that before one reaches the stage of asking, "What does it mean?" he must first concentrate on the discipline of ascertaining the answer to "What does it say?" The student should follow Agassiz's advice—"Look, look, look!"—and tarry long with the Biblical text itself be-

[12]Richard C. Trench, *Notes on the Parables of Our Lord* (London: Kegan Paul, Trench, and Co., 1889), p. 36.

fore resorting to other aids. This is the basic recommendation for inductive study of any part of the Bible and is, therefore, sound advice for study in the special areas of wisdom, parabolic, and apocalyptic literature.

Apocalyptic literature. Ezekiel, Daniel, and the Book of the Revelation are the apocalyptic books of the Bible. Apocalyptic writing is distinguished from prophetic writing in that the former is a presentation of a related succession of visions involving the last times, while prophecy is more a collection of various prophecies interwoven into a context of teaching, warning, and exhortation. Apocalyptic literature, unlike the prophetic books, abounds in figurative language—allegory, symbol, and type—and this creates one of the most difficult tasks of the Bible student.

Involved in the task of determining *what the author intended to say,* the student must determine, for example, what is symbolic and what is literal. This step alone, which must precede the hermeneutical question, What does it mean?, is at once crucial and difficult. One might say that there is a science of apocalyptic symbolism, an acquaintance with which is imperative for any student anticipating a thorough analysis of an apocalyptic book. Outside helps are a necessity for such an acquaintance. But again, the student can do much concentrated "looking" to see what is actually *in the text* in anticipation of determining what the text means. A large proportion of structural study can be pursued before a thorough acquaintance with the symbolical science is acquired.

B. What Does the Author Mean?

Determining what the author says and determining what the author means are the two study disciplines called observation and interpretation. For Bible study, knowing what the author actually says is to be well on the way to interpreting what he means.

A prerequisite for correct interpretation is correct observation. One does not hastily arrive at such correct interpretations. Even in the more simple passages of the Bible, the student must be willing to weigh all the evidence, as time-consuming as this process may be, being ever alert to that which is hidden behind the obvious. In other words, as Charles Eberhardt has well said,

> Interpretation must start . . . on the basis of a rigorous induction. Its work is at first painful and plodding. Whatever heights of vision there are beyond, the pathway necessarily must start here.[13]

The following essay, written by a ten-year-old pupil, amusingly illustrates a combination of correct observation, faulty observation, correct interpretation, and faulty interpretation:

> The Cow is a mammal. It has six sides—right, left, an upper and below. At the back it has a tail on which hangs a brush. With this it sends the flies away so that they do not fall into the milk. The head is for the purpose of growing horns and so that the mouth can be somewhere. The horns are to butt with, and the mouth is to moo with. Under the cow hangs the milk. It is arranged for milking. When people milk, the milk comes and there is never an end to the supply. How the cow does it I have not yet realized, but it makes more and more. . . . The man cow is called an ox. It is not a mammal. The cow does not eat much, but what it eats it eats twice, so that it gets enough. When it is hungry it moos, and when it says nothing it is because its inside is all full up with grass.[14]

That part of one's study procedure involving interpretation, which is the field of hermeneutics, is not a simple one. Textbooks on Biblical hermeneutics devote long sections to

[13]Eberhardt, op. cit., p. 187.
[14]Quoted by Edward Weeks, "The Peripatetic Reviewer," *The Atlantic Monthly*, Vol. 185 (June, 1950), p. 78.

general maxims as well as to special rules for such special types of writing as the parable and apocalypse. It is not the intention of this writer even to attempt to introduce the problems. The earnest Bible student will want to refer to good textbooks on the subject.[15]

One would be blind to the facts to presume that all parts of Scripture are easily interpreted or understood. As the Westminster Confession reads, "All things in Scripture are not alike plain in themselves, nor alike clear unto all." Charles Haddon Spurgeon said that when he faced those things which he could not understand, it seemed to him as though God had set a chair there for him to kneel down and worship. Surely the difficult and the obscure should be a challenge to fruitful study experiences. Furthermore, it is recognized that one may grasp a Biblical truth and still never fathom all of the implications of that truth. Who among men has exhausted all that is involved in Christ's atonement?

Nevertheless, most of the Bible is clear. Surely, as Bernard Ramm says, "Everything essential to salvation and Christian living is clearly revealed in Scripture."[16] This is accounted for in part by the fact that the comprehensiveness of the scope of the Bible allows it to be its best interpreter. Such self-interpretation involves cross-reference study, distant context reference, and, of greatest aid, the immediate or surrounding context. Since the inductive method of study which is being urged in these pages emphasizes this immediate context study, involving terms as well as structure, a studious devotion to the disciplines of this method is sure to aid the student in arriving at the true interpretation.

[15]For example, Milton Terry, *Biblical Hermeneutics* (Grand Rapids: Zondervan Publishing House, n.d.); Bernard Ramm, *Protestant Biblical Interpretation* (rev. ed., Boston: W. A. Wilde Co., 1956); and A. Berkeley Mickelsen, *Interpreting the Bible* (Grand Rapids: Wm. B. Eerdmans Pub. Co., 1963).
[16]Ramm, op. cit., p. 122.

C. How is the Message to be Applied?

Application is the end or goal of Bible study. This application involves the Bible student himself as the one acted upon. Not what *he* does to the Bible but what *It* does to *him* should be the student's main concern.

The application is usually conceived of as terminating in the life of the student himself. Actually, there is a further terminus, involving the student's *communication* to others. By way of recapitulation, then, Bible study involves the following:

1. Observation: What does it say?
2. Interpretation: What does it mean?
3. Application: How does it relate to me?
4. Communication: How do I give it to others?

In the observational and interpretive steps the student identifies the universal truth which is applicable to his time and situation. The option of heeding this truth or rejecting it involves the will of the student. This is the final test of the fruitfulness of the Bible study. There is no quantitative formula involving heart, mind, and body, the application of which guarantees such success. It is obvious that God has not placed a premium on spasmodic, inattentive, and hasty study of His Word. The Bible student will do well to take seriously the suggestion that methodicalness in the mental and physical disciplines of his Bible study is an intimate partner with such heart attitudes as receptiveness, humility, faith, and obedience. It is with this in mind that this writer is attempting to offer in the next pages some practical suggestions toward *a* practical method of studying the Bible.

CHAPTER III

THE ANALYTICAL CHART

ONE HESITATES to use the word "chart" in connection with Bible study because of the prejudices which have been built up against charts. Some object that a chart represents a mechanization of the spiritual. Others object that the chart suggests a blind dogmatism, or naïve exactness. Some shun the discipline of "chart-making" solely on the ground of the amount of work involved, while others avoid chart-making because of their supposed inability to work with diagrams.

The analytical chart method of study presented in this chapter has been warmly received by Bible students of varying ages, backgrounds, and achievement. Basically the chart represents the student's observations and interpretations of the Biblical text and is, therefore, hardly guilty of an anti-spiritual mechanization or narrow dogmatism. It is true that much work is involved in this method of study, but probably not any more work than is necessary for any intensive study of the Bible. Artistic ability is surely not a prerequisite for a successful application of the method, though facility in working *clearly* with pencil and paper is very desirable.

Any method which employs *writing down as one studies* has many virtues. Andrew Blackwood recognized this when he gave the following advice to anyone contemplating an intensive study of the Fourth Gospel:

> . . . the main stress ought to fall on reading the Bible book itself, as it was written, and on dealing with each paragraph as a unit. Before a man leaves any such literary unit, he

76

should be able to understand what it teaches about Christ in relation to other persons. Then he should *put down in black and white* the motif, or central teaching of the paragraph, in terms of Christ.[1]

Joseph M. Gettys, in his booklet, *Teaching Pupils How to Study the Bible,* gives this pertinent advice:

> You should stress to all of your pupils the importance of working on paper, for what is written on paper releases the mind to fasten its attention on something more.[2]

Now the primary value of the analytical chart lies in the fact that the student has extended his study to the point of graphically and clearly expressing his thoughts in black and white. The following represent some of the major values of the analytical chart:

I. VALUES OF AN ANALYTICAL CHART

A. Value of Keener Seeing

When Professor Agassiz said, "The pencil is one of the best eyes," he could not have placed a higher premium on such a simple mechanical device as the student's pencil. Of course he meant a pencil *in use*, for an unused pencil has no more practical worth than an unused eye. A Bible student, in a very real sense, has three study eyes. First and foremost, he has the eye of the Holy Spirit, one of whose major ministries to the Christian is that of illuminating the Scriptures. Without His guidance and teaching, the Bible would be one vast enigma to the Christian. Secondly, the Bible student has the physical eye with which to know God's written revelation. A man may have a Bible in every room of his house, but if he does not exercise his *eyes* to *read* the Word,

---

[1] Andrew W. Blackwood. "Giving Christ the Place of Honor," *Christianity Today,* IV (January 18, 1960), p. 7. Italics mine.
[2] Joseph M. Gettys, *Teaching Pupils How to Study the Bible* (Richmond: John Knox Press, 1950), p. 13.

he cannot expect the Word to reach him through some mystical operation. The third eye is the pencil. The interaction of the mental process of thinking thoughts and the physical process of writing down those thoughts must inevitably enlarge the field of vision for the student of the Bible.

B. Value of Retention and Permanence

1. *Retention*

William James once wrote that all normal minds have equal retentive powers and that they differ only in degrees of interest and methods of learning. While the truth of the former statement may be challenged, it is evident that the motivation of interest and the methods of learning have much to do with the amount of material which can be recalled at will some time after a study has been made. If it is approximately true that what one remembers is constituted of 50 percent saturation, 40 percent organization, and 10 percent pure memory, it is desirable for a student to use those methods of study which encourage organization of facts and utilize helps for saturation. The analytical chart method may be said to have both advantages. As for organization, the student is continually relating and integrating details and facts. As for saturation, the graphic method of recording one's study can claim the generally accepted statistics of the indelible impression of visual aids. Stated proverbially, "One picture is worth a thousand words."

2. *Permanence*

How often the student has experienced the frustration of vainly trying to recall an observation which he had made on a certain Scripture passage, because he had not jotted it down! The analytical chart method encourages the student, as each observation arises, always to JOT IT DOWN as a guarantee against lapse of memory. Further, whatever the student writes on paper is in at least semipermanent form, to be referred to for the years to come, or to be revised and expanded by later supplementary studies.

C. Value of Seeing the Whole Simultaneously

The common error of failing to see the forest because of the pressing closeness of the multitude of trees is committed very often in Bible study. Someone has said, "These are times in which whatsoever is of boundless dimensions in Holy Scripture has passed beyond our range of vision while our spectacled eyes are on iotas." Any study discipline or method which attempts to keep before the student's eyes the whole in relation to each of the parts, is a forward step in minimizing the tendency to bog down in "the quagmires of detail." Stability of interpretation demands that the student always see the guiding star in the overall structure of the passage.

The analytical chart method is designed to keep the major body of the student's recording on one side of a standard sheet of paper, 8½ by 11 inches. Within a defined area on the page the entire text of the passage under study is clearly printed or written, with the marginal spaces being used for such items as observational notes and outlines. Thus for each unit of study the beginning and the end and all that is between is continually and simultaneously before the student's eye.

D. Value of Integrating the Various Parts

In the Bible, things purposefully "hook and eye together." It is the student's task to take of the many facts, ideas, and doctrines contained within one segment of study, and discover the integrated or woven designs.

The analytical chart permits ease and clarity of recording (and observing) the student's integrated studies in the following ways:

1. Word studies may be recorded within the text, or in the margin.

2. Topical studies may be outlined in the margins opposite the occurrence of the respective thoughts in the text, each individual study being kept distinct from all others.

3. Progressions, contrasts, comparisons, and focal points are easily recorded in the marginal spaces. For example, by drawing a line from the first words of a passage to the last, the student may be pointing to a contrast, or comparison. If the relation is not obvious, he can indicate the relation in the margin.

4. A key thought, with its relation to each paragraph, can be made dominant on the analytical chart, and can indicate the vantage point from which the study is being made.

The major advantage of the analytical chart with respect to integration is the fact that numerous outlines, word studies, and the like may be recorded on one page with a minimum of confusion. The logical outline is another type of valuable integration, but its disadvantage lies in the fact that many important studies are either forfeited or obscured by the very limitations of the one continuous outline. For example, a student who outlines a passage of Scripture using the standard outline form—I, A, 1, *a*, (1), (*a*), etc.—methodically progresses to the end of the passage without backtracking in the text. Any supplementary outline studies on the same passage cannot be superimposed on the master outline. The analytical chart, on the other hand, allows the student flexibility in simultaneously recording various outlines in a coherent and attractive manner.

E. Value of Emphasizing the Primary Over the Subordinate

The analytical chart, when it is made clearly and correctly, distinguishes what is primary and what is subordinate through the use of such various means as large print, bold print, underlining, circling, and the use of color pencils. The use of such visual aids during the process of study is a fruitful discipline, for it demands that the student be continually alert in evaluating the relative importance of each minute part of his study with reference to other parts and the whole.

F. Value of a Visually Defined Area of Study

Methodicalness and efficiency are musts for effective Bible study. Translating one's thinking to a written condensed record on the defined area of an analytical chart is one way of minimizing such study faults as haphazardness, undefined goals, haziness as to relations of parts, and external distractions. The construction of a visual analytical chart by its very nature incites (1) concentration of thought within a defined Scripture passage, (2) explicit identification of the aims of both Biblical writer and students, (3) continual association of parts, and (4) a minimum of external distractions.

G. Value of Training in Communication

As stated previously, from the practical standpoint there are two termini of Bible study, one in the student's life, the other in the lives of others to whom the student communicates Bible truth. It is one thing to be able to study efficiently and understand the Bible; it is another thing to be able to teach others, or communicate one's understanding to others. Any study discipline which develops in the student the technique of expression and communication is therefore very vital. In the construction of an analytical chart the student is continually re-creating, recasting, condensing, synchronizing, and clarifying, as he translates his thoughts into the verbal, into the black and white, into the visible record. The chart demands visible expression; and the experience of so expressing, in communicative form, one's thought processes is essential training for the one who desires to teach others.

This of course is not to imply that the deep spiritual truths can be *fully* described by the student in writing. A man would not attempt *any* verbal communication of the spiritual message if the prior requirement were exhaustive understanding of the eternal spiritual truths. But insofar as one's mental and spiritual apprehension of a Biblical truth can be expressed verbally, the analytical chart method is one of the finest methods designed to train the Christian in this vital ministry of teaching.

II. THE STUDENT AND HIS EQUIPMENT

"Where do I begin?" would be a normal question asked by the interested "apprentice" who desires to study the Bible inductively by use of the analytical chart method. The logical beginning place is *the student himself*, for ultimately *he* holds the key to all fruitful Bible study.

A. The Student

1. *Dependence on the Holy Spirit*

Methodical Bible study cannot be truly effective Bible study without the active illuminating ministry of the Holy Spirit. Robert Traina said, "He who inspired the Word is also its supreme interpreter."[3] Two extreme attitudes are to be avoided regarding the Holy Spirit's ministry. The first is that of an extreme passivity in which the student avoids the disciplines of toil and sweat and equates Bible study only with an "inner voice" teaching him. The other error is associated with an intense mental activity, involving much time and study, in which the Spirit's illuminating ministry is not recognized or received. It is obvious that effective Bible

[3]Robert Traina, *Methodical Bible Study* (privately published, 1952) p. 13.

study involves the combined activities of both the student and the Holy Spirit.

If the earnest Bible student comes to the Scriptures in reverence, being continually aware of his need for help and of God's offer for help, he will find himself engaged in fruitful labor. What Andrew Murray said about the disciples' prayer, "Lord, teach us to pray," is especially applicable to the attitude of the Bible student:

> Let . . . the deep undertone of all our prayer be the teachableness that comes from a *sense of ignorance*. . . .[4]

W. W. White gives the following three "laws of the heart," which adequately sum up the spiritual attitude of the Bible student:

1. *The Law of Prayer:* The Word of God can be adequately understood only through communion with God. So, let us constantly use prayer as a means of Bible study.
2. *The Law of the Holy Spirit:* The Holy Spirit has been given to reveal to us the deep things of God. Therefore, let us continually seek His illumination.
3. *The Law of Our Spiritual Nature:* Our spiritual natures have the capacity and the ability to respond to God's truths. We must, therefore, trust Him and act promptly upon impressions which we are certain come from Him through the Holy Spirit as we read His Word.

2. Basic Attitudes

Recognition of the Bible's authority. A deep conviction of the authority and infallibility of the Scriptures is of paramount importance for the Bible student. The very words (verbal) and all the words (plenary), of the original writings must be recognized, in faith, as infallible.

Such a conviction or faith is not without adequate basis.

[4]Andrew Murray, *With Christ in the School of Prayer* (New York: Fleming H. Revell Co., n.d.), p. 5. Italics mine.

It is based first of all on the Bible's own witness to itself. For example, every Scripture was God-breathed (II Tim. 3:16). It is based also on the flawless character of the One who moved the men to write, for they spake as they were moved by the Holy Spirit (II Pet. 1:21). The authority of the Scriptures also comes from the lips of the Son of God who, as someone has put it, accredited the Old Testament retrospectively (Luke 24:44), and the New Testament prospectively (e.g., John 14:26; 16:13).

Furthermore, this *witness* of the Bible's authority has its *confirmation* in the Bible's history. From its original production to its becoming a very part of the individual lives of God's people today, the Bible represents a series of miracles.

It is a miracle as to its birth, as inscrutable as God's creation of the first man, Adam.

It is a miracle as to its individual parts *growing* into one unit, called the canon, without any one individual or group officially decreeing the bounds of that canon. The stamp of the supernatural authority of God was so indelibly impressed upon only the *inspired* books that by the time of Christ all the books of the Old Testament were recognized by the people of God as the body of Scriptures, and by A.D. 400 the twenty-seven books of the present New Testament stood aloft as the remainder of God's writings.

It is a miracle as to its *transmission* through the thousands of scribal copyings into the era of modern printing. When we consider the human frailties of eye, ear, and memory which would normally jeopardize the accuracy of any early manuscript copied by a scribe from another manuscript, and when we recognize the fantastic proportions to which a small inaccuracy could easily grow in the hundreds of generations of copyings, we cannot help but conclude that the substantially pure text of our versions today is explained only by one fact: God's miraculous superintendence.

It is a miracle as to its *translation* from the original languages into the vernaculars. What causes an Indian, after reading an Indian version of the Bible, to remark that this book was *always* written in his language? What brings that same impression to us regarding our English version? For this and other reasons we see the miracle hand of God in translation.

The divine source of the Bible—and therefore its authority—is seen also in its miraculous *preservation*. All writings are eventually exposed to those elements that would deprive them of their very existence. As for the Bible, straying, disuse, fire, and rot could not destroy it. Today the rationalistic attempts of the liberal scholars to explain it away have failed, and it still transforms hearts through its message of the Grand Miracle: Eternal Life.

With such a deep conviction of the divine authority of the Scriptures, the student is on solid ground motivation-wise. He will not question the inclusion in the Bible of certain passages just because they are difficult or obscure; he will not react to the Book as a man to the voice of a man; he will not come to the Scriptures with suspicion. Instead, he will enter the sanctuary of the Word knowing that here is the "thus saith the Lord," here are the oracles of God, here is Truth itself, divinely garbed in the clothing of human language. He MUST come away a different man.

Receptivity. It was W. W. White's advice to "table all presuppositions and questions" while one searches the materials at hand. The student should read to be impressed, letting the impressions ripen into convictions. He should not come to the Bible with the thought of doing something to it, but rather of letting it do something to him. The attitude of expectancy with which one anticipates the portentous arrival of an important messenger is a healthy attitude. It has been said that "whoso seeketh an interpretation *from* this book shall get an answer from God; whoso bringeth an interpretation *to* it shall get an answer from the devil." The spirit of receptivity, then, is a must for the Bible student.

Will. There are many distractions and temptations for anyone engaged in Bible study. He who has a *will* to study, and guards it with all his might, has strong defense. And how much the Bible discloses to him who is determined to learn! J. H. Jowett once wrote, "Get a will behind the eye, and the eye becomes a searchlight, the familiar is made to disclose undreamed treasure."[5]

Exactness. Slovenliness is inexcusable in Bible study. Exacting care must be exercised in observing what the Bible says. Mortimer J. Adler recognizes in the following description an intense exactness in reading on the part of one who has just received a love letter:

> If we consider men and women generally, and apart from their professions or occupations, there is only one situation I can think of in which they almost pull themselves up by their bootstraps, making an effort to read better than they usually do. When they are in love and are reading a love letter, they read for all they are worth. They read every word three ways; they read between the lines and in the margins; they read the whole in terms of the parts, and each part in terms of the whole; they grow sensitive to context and ambiguity, to insinuation and implication; they perceive the color of words, the odor of phrases, and the weight of sentences. They may even take the punctuation into account. Then, if never before or after, they read.[6]

The application to Bible study is obvious.

Professor Agassiz appealed especially to exactness and concentrated observation in one's study of a fish.[6a] Surely no

---

[5] J. H. Jowett, *Brooks by the Traveller's Way* (New York: George H. Doran Co., n.d.), pp. 78, 79.

[6] Mortimer J. Adler, *How to Read a Book* (New York: Simon and Schuster, Inc., Pub., 1940), p. 14.

[6a] See Appendix II.

lesser concentration should characterize the study of the Bible.

3. Fresh Approach

Physically speaking, the best hours for study come when the body is in keenest fitness, not when the body is weary from the responsibilities of the day.

From a mental and psychological standpoint, a student should approach a passage of Scripture with as moldable an outlook as possible. For example, by not reading commentaries about the passage *before* studying the passage itself, he will avoid "reducing the threshold of perception by prejudicing the mind."[7] Also, his first studies in the passage should be in a text which has not been underlined, annotated or marked during previous studies. As much as possible, he should approach the passage as though he had never seen it before, for without this check the oft read phrase all too easily becomes trite or unimpressive. How often has the rhythmically read "verily, verily" lost its impact because of its familiar sound!

From a spiritual standpoint, it is obvious that spiritual dearth, confusion, or ungenuineness are devastating to a keen perception of scriptural truth. Horace Bushnell once observed:

> My experience is that the Bible is dull when I am dull. When I am really alive and set upon the text with a tidal pressure of living affinities, it opens, it multiplies discoveries, and reveals depths even faster than I can note them.[8]

The student's approach to the Bible should be as keen and excitedly expectant as that of the explorer who gazes for the first time into a hitherto undiscovered cave. And what is

[7]Traina, op. cit., p. 25.
[8]Quoted in Traina, op. cit., p. 13.

more, the Bible student may have the assurance beforehand that the Scripture upon which he intently gazes always contains a mine of eternal gems, waiting to be found and owned!

4. *Toil and Sweat*

Just as it has been said concerning prayer that "prayer is work, and prayer works," so it may be said concerning thorough Bible study, "Bible study is work; Bible study works."

There are at least *four misconceptions* held by some concerning this aspect of Bible study. They are:

Effective Bible study need not involve much work. It is true that many spiritual blessings may be experienced daily by the Christian as he quietly, briefly, and in relaxed mood meditates over a short passage of Scripture. But considering the Bible as a whole, and involving all types of passages —the obvious and the obscure, the short and the long, the historical and the doctrinal, the poetical and the apocalyptic, and the literal and the figurative—it is obvious that a thorough analysis of such passages, whatever methods are employed, must involve toil and sweat, perseverance and patience.

There is no shortcut to effective Bible study. The student who expects to be spoon-fed by his teacher or by the author of the commentary is deluding himself into thinking that he is really studying the passage, for both of these aids are rather intended to incite study motivation, via direction, suggestion, and inspiration. Professor John A. Leighton, in *The Field of Philosophy*, says of Socrates:

> If Socrates were here today, he would doubtless say that much of what we call knowledge he would call degraded knowledge, or even not knowledge at all. Our handing out of cold storage pablum to blindly-accepting pupils is not the true way of imparting and acquiring knowledge. Knowledge for Socrates was personal insight which men

acquire by their own persistent activity. . . . We find no peptenized, predigested, after-breakfast knowledge tablets in Socrates. Belief must cost the sweat of the intellectual brow, or it is not knowledge.[9]

Someone has very aptly remarked that Socrates conceived it to be his function not to impart to students what he thought, but to "bring to birth their conclusions." So, in the final analysis, for best results, there is no shortcut to study—the student must be willing to do most of the work himself.

What is tedious is unimportant. The fallacy of this misconception is illustrated on every hand. The performance of the concert pianist in Carnegie Hall is *the* great event, the climax to many a dream. But the long, tedious hours and years of practice and study prior to the appearance are not therefore considered to be unimportant. The simplicity of Einstein's tremendous energy-matter formula, $E = mc^2$, does not imply a simple and fascinating quality about all of Einstein's hours and years of research leading up to such a discovery.

Some may object that the method of studying a scriptural passage by an analytical chart is purely mechanical, involving much that is tedious and therefore not a method to be seriously considered. It is the earnest desire of this writer that the reader will not equate the mechanical and the tedious with the unimportant or the unfruitful.[10]

Clarity is always that which is obvious at first sight. Not so. Has it not often happened that a student of the Bible has pondered *long* over a phrase or passage before his exclamation, "*Now* I see it!" What was not obvious at first sight becomes radiantly bright and clear after long study. Havelock Ellis refers to such a process as moving from obscurity to clarity. Referring this process to the study of a great masterpiece, he says,

[9]John A. Leighton, *The Field of Philosophy* (New York: Appleton-Century-Crofts, Inc., 1930).
[10]Cf. Traina, op. cit., p. 18.

The impression we receive upon first entering the presence of any supreme work of art is obscurity. But it is an obscurity like that of a Catalonian cathedral which slowly grows luminous as one gazes until the solid structure beneath is revealed. The veil of its depth grows first transparent in the form of art before our eyes, then the veil of its beauty, and at last there is only clarity.[11]

There are many factors entering into the metamorphosis of obscurity to clarity, and two of these may be cited at this point. First, the student's spiritual perception of the Holy Scriptures, God's Revelation, depends on the ministry of the Holy Spirit, the Revelator, for, as Ellis says, "There must be a correspondence between an object and the organ to which it reveals itself."[12] Secondly, the student must be willing to spend *much time* with the Scripture passage. The hasty impatient student would not make a good student of Professor Agassiz. Clarence E. Flynn writes about the patient gaze thus:

> Peering into the mists of gray
> That shroud the surface of the bay,
> Nothing I see except a veil
> Of fog surrounding every sail.
> Then suddenly against a cape
> A vast and silent form takes shape,
> A great ship lies against the shore
> Where nothing has appeared before.
>
> Who sees a truth must often gaze
> Into a fog for many days;
> It may seem very sure to him
> Nothing is there but mist-clouds dim.
> Then, suddenly, his eyes will see
> A shape where nothing used to be.

[11]Havelock Ellis, *Impressions and Comments* (Boston: Houghton Mifflin Co., 1929).
[12]Ibid.

Discoveries are missed each day
By men who turn too soon away.[13]

The Bible is exhaustible. This fourth misconception short circuits Bible study-in-depth. How disturbing it would be if it were true that after a study through the circuit of the Bible's sixty-six books there was nothing new to learn or teach. Streaming from the eternal fountainhead, the Bible by its very nature can never be exhausted. As the Christian grows in spiritual stature and acumen through his constant study of the Word, even so he is enabled to perceive more deeply and more fully in his subsequent studies. As Traina says, "Our personal growth enables us to find more in the Scriptures tomorrow than we found today."[14] The never-ending publications of new Bible commentaries by various authors, much of the contents of which are not mere duplication, is mute evidence of the fact that men are still seeing new and wonderful truths in the Book.

* * *

So Bible study is work. But it is blessed work, and fruitful. It is not to be engaged in purely for the sake of scholarship, for, as James Russell Lowell has said, "there is nothing less fruitful than scholarship for the sake of mere scholarship, nor anything more wearisome in the attainment."[15] But no higher motivation can be attributed to Bible study than when it is pursued with the earnest and humble desire for a more intimate knowledge of Him who is

the blessed and only Potentate,
the King of kings, and Lord of lords;
who only hath immortality,
dwelling in light unapproachable;

13Quoted in Traina, op. cit., p. 33.
14Traina, op. cit., p. 21.
15Quoted from "541," May, 1915, published by the students of The Biblical Seminary in New York.

whom no man hath seen, nor can see:
to whom be honor and power eternal.

(I Tim. 6:15-16, A.S.V.)

B. Equipment

The analytical chart method described in these pages understandably involves some equipment in addition to the text of the Bible itself. The list of that equipment is kept to a minimum here.

1. *The Holy Bible*

The student is strongly urged to do the major part of his concentrated study in *one* version of the Bible, reserving reference to any other versions to a later stage in the study process. In doing so the student's mental picture of the unit of study can thus be more indelibly impressed and defined in the first fresh stages of study, when such impressions should be made. To bring into view from the outset a multitude of translations, interpretations, and word studies is only to invite mental confusion and obscurity in perspective. Concentration, followed by expansion, is the rule of procedure here.

a. The Mother Tongue

For the English-speaking student, the English Bible should be the basic study text. Dr. Kuist correctly observes that "the mother tongue is the most effective instrument of learning because it is the medium in which he [the student] thinks best."[16] And especially for this inductive method of study which involves the recognition of the broad structural relations, the mother tongue enables one to see these rela-

[16]Howard Tillman Kuist, Introductory Lectures in Pauline Epistles, given at The Biblical Seminary in New York, January, 1947, quoted in Eberhardt, op. cit., p. 106.

tions in a way virtually impossible for the average student using the original languages.[17]

It is true that the well-trained exegete who is skilled in the rapid reading of Greek or Hebrew can grasp those broad structural relations in the Biblical languages. It may be observed here, however, that many Greek and Hebrew teachers are aware of the major weakness of some of the standard grammar books being used for beginning Greek and Hebrew classes—that is, that concentration is on *grammar* at the expense of some facility to *read,* in the correct sense of the term.

Henry R. Moeller identifies this weakness of such grammar books thus:

> The process by which one takes the rules given in a descriptive grammar, along with a lexicon, and laboriously deciphers a text word by word and point by grammatical point is *not* reading. Yet it is the level of competence to which many students have been brought after a whole academic year of fairly intensive grammar study. It is also a way to cripple potential exegetes in process of birth.[18]

Reading, says Dr. Moeller, involves the "recognition of the meanings *not* of words as *words,* but of words *in significant orders of arrangement and of constructional relationships.*"[19]

For the average Bible student, it still holds true that reading in the mother tongue makes one most aware of those constructional relationships. Actually, for such a student it is later on in the study process that he should refer to the original languages, indirectly or otherwise; and then such references usually involve word studies, such as etymology, comparative philology, case, and tense, rather than

[17]See Traina, op. cit., p. 9.
[18]Henry R. Moeller, "An Approach to the Greek Reading Problem Based on Structural Statistics," *Bulletin of the Evangelical Theological Society* (Spring, 1960), p. 45.
[19] Ibid.

structural studies. At that stage of one's study, word studies in the original languages bring out the detail and color resident in the Biblical author's words.

b. A Bible Version for Analytical Study

Analytical study calls for a Bible version which is an exact translation of the original languages, retaining as much as possible the style, structure, and word length of the autographs, with a minimum of free paraphrasing. One reason for not using a paraphrase version for firsthand analysis is that it is the paraphraser's interpretation of the Bible text; and interpretation is what the Bible student aims to arrive at himself, in the very process of analysis.[20]

The *New American Standard Bible* (NASB)[21] is recommended for the inductive method of study described in these pages, first, because it is an accurate translation with little paraphrasing. The style and structure of the autographs are adequately retained, and generally a minimal number of English words are used to translate each Hebrew or Greek word.[22a] Concerning style and vocabulary, the translators were careful not to succumb to "the ever-present danger of stripping divine Truth of its dignity and original intent."[22b]

The NASB is basically a revision of the American Standard Version (ASV) of 1901.[22c] The latter version had been (and still is) recognized as an excellent text for Bible analysis. So the purpose of the editorial board in revising the ASV included preserving all the valuable qualities of the text, and

---

[20]All versions, including KJV, have some paraphrases, since some words of the original text, such as idioms, do not allow for a literal translation.

[21]*New American Standard Bible* (Chicago: Moody). Copyright by the Lockman Foundation, 1960, 1962, 1963, 1968, 1971, 1972, 1973, 1975.

[22a]Even without paraphrasing, it often takes more than one English word to translate one Hebrew or Greek word, simply because of the ancient languages' multisyllable word construction. For example, the syllables of the single Greek word *gnorisai* require the infinitive translation of three words, "to make known."

[22b]Preface, NASB.

[22c]*The Holy Bible,* Standard Edition (New York: Thomas Nelson & Sons, 1901). The ASV is an American revision of the King James Version.

adding improvements, such as clear and contemporary language, which would enhance the version. The different kinds of improvements are described in the introductory pages of NASB. Bible students who had been using ASV for analysis before NASB appeared are now finding NASB to be a very excellent text for this type of Bible study.

The NASB is also recommended for analytical study because of the format of its pages. In many editions of the NASB, the Bible text is printed in one wide column, which keeps complete phrases intact more often than does the narrow-column format. It is unfortunate that each verse is printed as a new paragraph, but this need not hinder paragraph analysis as long as the student is continually aware of a chapter's "thought units." (The beginning of each thought unit is indicated in NASB by boldface numbers of the verses.) The Reference Edition of NASB is especially recommended for Bible students. It contains valuable marginal notes, verse cross-references, and blank spaces for recording notations.

There are a few other versions besides the NASB and ASV whose text is of the analytical-study type. Among these are the New Berkeley Version[22d], the Revised Standard Version[22e], the New International Version[22f], and the King James Version. All of these versions are available in paragraph format, which is very helpful for the analysis process.[22g] The New Berkeley Version uses two columns of Bible text on a page rather than the preferred one-column format; and the New International Version clearly identifies study segments but obscures paragraphical thought-units in the conversations of narrative passages.

[22d]*The Holy Bible,* The New Berkeley Version (Grand Rapids: Zondervan, 1969).

[22e]*The Holy Bible,* Revised Standard Version (New York: Thomas Nelson & Sons, 1952).

[22f]*The Holy Bible,* New International Version, New Testament (Grand Rapids: Zondervan, 1973).

[22g]The following two editions of the King James Version print the Bible text in paragraphic form: The Westminster Study Edition of the Holy Bible (Philadelphia: Westminster, 1958); and the New Reference Bible (New York: American Bible Society, 1963).

2. Paper

A few simple practical suggestions about materials for recording are in order here.

The student will want to use two types of paper, an inexpensive type for rough scratch work, and a better heavy quality paper for permanent recording. Both types should be of the large standard notebook size, 8½ by 11 inches. The permanent-type paper may be either ruled or unruled, but if the former, the rulings should be very light-colored.

Writing Tools

Since the final draft of the analytical chart should be in a quasi-permanent form, the use of a pen is suggested for printing. And since it is very desirable that words and phrases printed on the analytical chart be distinguished one from the other as to importance or relation to other parts of the passage, the use of various colors of ink is recommended. The writer has found many types of ball-point pens in colors of green, red, blue, and black to be very suitable. When using ball-point pens it is suggested that the student always rest his writing hand over a small piece of paper between his hand and the analytical chart to prevent any hand moisture, which always contains an element of oil, from being transferred to the analytical chart, thus making some ball-point script very uneven and, sometimes, unintelligible.

For recording preliminary observations on scratch notepaper, an ordinary pencil with black lead is sufficient. A Scripto pencil with red lead is very useful for making notations in the Bible text itself, or for printing and underlining on the analytical chart. In addition to these two standard pencils, it is highly recommended that the student use for his finished analytical chart a good set of color pencils. As has been mentioned already, one of the crucial tasks of the Bible student, whatever method he may use to study the

Bible, is to evaluate words and phrases as to what is primary and what is subordinate and to relate words and phrases within a passage to each other as far as the Biblical author's intentions can be reconstructed. In recording such evaluations or relations on the analytical chart, any graphic devices which may serve such a purpose—such as underlining, printing in various sizes of type, circling, using different colors, and using arrows—should be used. For purposes of clarity, however, any one graphic device should not be overdone; the employment of many such devices is very desirable. The use of color pencils in printing, shading areas, circling, drawing arrows, and underlining, therefore, constitutes a major part of one's *mechanical* construction of the analytical chart.

Purely for the sake of neatness, a straightedge is suggested for drawing the large rectangle, underlining long phrases, and drawing long arrows.

4. *Outside Helps*

As has been suggested earlier, the time for recourse to outside helps for amplification or correction purposes is in the *later* stages of one's study of a Scripture passage.

A further suggestion is in order here. Since the most important part of the analytical chart is the record of that which the student has seen firsthand for himself, it is vital that he become proficient in this discipline first. Therefore it is suggested that the student do a series of analyses *without the outside-help phase* at all, to the point where it becomes a usual pattern for him to compose an analytical chart with a substantial amount of original marginal studies before going to outside aids. The students of this writer's classes, before being encouraged to use aids, make approximately twenty analytical charts and use only the Bible text, thus becoming thoroughly ingrained with the facility of original study.

When the time has come for the student to amplify and supplement his own firsthand study, there is a variety of aids at his call, such as background materials, various versions, word studies and commentaries.

a. Background Reference Books

Much background material, involving such things as history, geography, culture, and authorship of books of Scripture, may be found in Bible dictionaries, Bible atlases, Bible history books, works on archaeology, and introductory guides to the two testaments. The frequency of one's reference to such books will depend on the type of Scriptural passage being analyzed.

b. Other Versions

It was mentioned earlier that the student should concentrate his analysis on the text of *one* version of the Bible, and refer to other versions at later stages in the study process. The main purpose of referring to such auxiliary versions (translations or paraphrases) is to clarify the meanings of words and phrases and, in the case of strongly idiomatic versions, to get the general intent of the phrases and sentences. In the case of some of the more amplified translations, much of the detail and color of the Hebrew and Greek words are preserved. This is possible because the translators have not been restricted by word economy, but are free to expand a word to convey a full meaning. Kenneth Wuest's expanded translations are examples of such representations.

Individual versions are not without their shortcomings. Such weaknesses may relate to the text itself, to the theological or professional qualifications of the editorial committee, or to such mechanical things as format, print, binding, cost, and the like. Translation shortcomings in the text itself are the ones about which the student is ultimately concerned. The comparative use of at least three or four good versions is a rather dependable check on a possible misrepresentation (as slight as it may be) of a Biblical word or phrase by one version.

(1) Entire Bible

The King James Version. F. F. Bruce says that if the student wants "a literary masterpiece, with old haunting associations and beautiful cadences," he will prefer the King James Version.[23] Because this Authorized Version is probably the version with which the student is most familiar, it can be of much value for reference work. As already noted, however, it is not readily available in paragraphic form. The format of each-verse-a-block often obscures the flow of the author's original writing. Actually the King James text is very suitable for analytical study, since it is a translation, not a paraphrase, and is written in such an excellent literary style.[24]

New American Standard Bible. Refer to pages 94-95 for a description of this recommended version.

New International Version (NIV). The New Testament of NIV appeared in 1973; the Old Testament is scheduled for publication in 1978. Three values of this version are its accuracy, readability, and very clear one-column format.

The New Berkeley Version in Modern English. One of the more recent modern versions of the entire Bible is *The New Berkeley Version* (1969).[25] The New Testament, which first appeared in 1945, was the work of Gerrit Verkuyl; and the Old Testament, which first appeared in 1959, is essentially the work of twenty scholars. The revised edition of 1969 mainly reflects revisions of the New Testament. F. F. Bruce regards this version as a masterpiece of evangelical scholarship. One of the main features of format in this Bible is the division of the text into short paragraphs.

Revised Standard Version. The Revised Standard Version

---

[23]F. F. Bruce, *The Books and the Parchments.* 3d ed. (Westwood, N. J.: Fleming H. Revell Co., 1963), p. 233.

[24]The King James Version is the basic study text used in the Bible Self-Study Guide series written by this author (Moody Press). Modern versions are consulted regularly for their vital aid.

[25]*The Holy Bible, The New Berkeley Version* (Rev. ed.; Grand Rapids: Zondervan Publishing House, 1969).

(New Testament, 1946; entire Bible, 1952[26]) is a revision of the American Standard Version. Its format is very similar to the Berkeley version. The *Harper Study Bible*, a study edition of the Revised Standard Version, edited by Harold Lindsell, is valuable for its introductions to each book, marginal references, and "interpretive notes written from the standpoint of conservative theological scholarship."[27]

The Moffatt Translation. James Moffatt's translation,[28] the New Testament section of which first appeared in 1913, is recognized by many to be a pivotal work in the development of modern versions. Its major weakness, that of an excessively free and idiomatic representation of the original text, points to its major value, that of giving the student the general drift of the larger movements of the text. Bruce says, "To read through one of the New Testament epistles in Moffatt's version is one of the best ways of getting a grasp of the general argument."[29]

Amplified Bible. The Amplified Bible,[30] which also represents the textual research of mainly one person, is intended primarily for Bible study, not for public reading. Alternate readings or explanations which would normally appear as footnotes are incorporated in the text with the use of parentheses and brackets. The light which these amplified readings throw on the verbs, nouns, prepositions, and various grammatical constructions, in accordance with the original language, is a valuable aid to the Bible student.

New English Bible. The *New English Bible*[31] (N. T. 1961; O. T. 1970) represents the work of a host of biblical scholars of Great Britain. Its English style has been described as

[26]*The Holy Bible, Revised Standard Version* (New York: Thomas Nelson and Sons, 1952).

[27]*Harper Study Bible*, Revised Standard Version, edited by Harold Lindsell (New York: Harper and Row Publishers, 1964), p. xiv.

[28]James Moffatt, translator, *The Bible, A New Translation* (New York: Harper and Brothers Publishers, 1922, 1935, 1950).

[29]Bruce, op. cit., p. 235.

[30]*The Amplified Bible* (Grand Rapids: Zondervan Publishing House, 1965).

[31]*The New English Bible* (Oxford: Oxford University Press, 1970).

"idiomatic yet elegant." Its format is that of paragraphs, with the text extending from margin to margin.

The Living Bible. The first section of this easy-to-read paraphrase[32] by Kenneth N. Taylor appeared in 1962 as *Living Letters.* It is similar in style and purpose to J. B. Phillips's paraphrase of the New Testament. It is especially valuable for clarifying deep and difficult passages of the Bible. Whenever interpretations are supplied by the author, they are from an evangelical viewpoint.

(2) New Testament Only

Williams's Translation. The New Testament in The Language of The People,[33] by Charles B. Williams, which was first published by Moody Press in 1949, has special value for the student interested in an amplified expression of the Greek verb tenses, which are not always obvious in some versions. As an example, compare these two translations of Philippians 4:6:

> In nothing *be* anxious; but . . . let your requests *be made* known unto God (American Standard Version).

> *Stop being* worried about anything, but . . . *keep on making* your wants known to God (Williams).

Weymouth's Translation. Richard F. Weymouth's *The New Testament in Modern Speech,*[34] the first edition of which appeared in 1902, is similar to William's translation in accentuating the Greek verb tenses.

Goodspeed's Translation. Edgar J. Goodspeed's translation first appeared in 1923.[35] It is very similar to Weymouth's version in format and content. The speech of Weymouth's ver-

[32]Kenneth N. Taylor, *The Living Bible* (Wheaton, Illinois: Tyndale House Publishers, 1971).

[33]Charles B. Williams, translator, *The New Testament in The Language of The People* (Chicago: Moody Press, 1952).

[34]Richard F. Weymouth, translator, *The New Testament in Modern Speech* (5th ed.; New York: Harper and Brothers, 1929).

[35]Edgar J. Goodspeed, translator, *New Testament* (Chicago: University of Chicago Press, 1923).

sion is directed especially to the British, while Goodspeed's version is with the American reader in mind.

Phillips's Paraphrase. The New Testament in Modern English[36] by J. B. Phillips is a paraphrase, intended, as the author says in his preface to *Letters to Young Churches*, to have an "easy-to-read" quality.[37] The major value of this version is in its maintaining a continuous relatedness of each verse to each succeeding verse within each paragraph. "For close meticulous study," advises Dr. Phillips, "existing modern versions should be consulted."[38]

Wuest's Translation. Kenneth S. Wuest's *The New Testament: An Expanded Translation*[39] is another valuable aid to the Bible student. The translation is really an English expansion of the Greek text intended to give the full equivalent of such things as Greek tenses, the use of articles, the order of words, etc.

Today's English Version. Also known as *Good News for Modern Man,*[40] this popular translation seeks to express the meaning of the Greek text in common, everyday English phraseology. Its underlying purpose is to make the Bible text simple and clear, as readable as a daily newspaper. The version might be classified between simplified translation and condensed paraphrase. The entire Old Testament is scheduled for publication in 1976.

c. Word Studies

The study of single Bible words, weighing them to determine their content and function, can be a very fascinating exercise in the analysis of a passage. Wilbur M. Smith writes,

[36]J. B. Phillips, translator, *The New Testament in Modern English* (New York: The Macmillan Company, 1953).

[37]J. B. Phillips, *Letters to Young Churches* (New York: The Macmillan Company, 1950), p. xi.

[38]*Ibid.*

[39]Kenneth S. Wuest, translator, *The New Testament: An Expanded Translation* (Grand Rapids: William B. Eerdmans Publishing Co., 1961).

[40]*The New Testament in Today's English Version* (New York: American Bible Society, 1966).

"There is no book in the world whose words will yield such treasures of truth, such spiritual richness, such rivers of refreshing water, such strengthening of the soul as the words with which the Holy Spirit inspired the authors of the books of our Bible."[40a]

There are two basic areas of studying a Bible word: (1) learning how the particular word is used in Scripture; and (2) learning the word's literal meaning.

Help in the first type of study is offered by cross-references in the margins of the Bible, which cite other passages using the same word, and by an exhaustive concordance, which shows every passage in the Bible where the particular word appears.[41]

Sources which treat the literal meanings of Bible words include concordances of the type mentioned above,[42] and such works as W. E. Vine's *An Expository Dictionary of New Testament Words*.[43]

The books mentioned above are invaluable aids to the student in that they concentrate on giving the background, etymology, and current and comparative uses of words in both biblical and secular usage. Good commentaries, which treat the text of the original languages, also offer many excellent word studies.

d. Commentaries

Last, and by no means least, the student will want to have access to good commentaries, especially those whose authors have worked with the original languages of the text. If commentary reference is made toward the end of one's

[40a]Wilbur M. Smith, *Profitable Bible Study* (Boston: W. A. Wilde Co., 1939), p. 43.

[41]A recommended concordance is James Strong, *The Exhaustive Concordance of the Bible* (New York: Abingdon, 1890). A similar work is Robert Young, *Analytical Concordance to the Bible* (Grand Rapids: William B. Eerdmans Publishing Co., n.d.).

[42]In Strong's concordance this information appears at the back of the volume.

[43]W. E. Vine, *An Expository Dictionary of New Testament Words* (Westwood, N. J.: Fleming H. Revell Co., 1961).

study of a passage—when such reference should be made—much of what the commentary presents will have been already observed by the student in his independent study. The special values of the commentary, in addition to its introductory materials, are its treatment of the problem passages, its casting of the historical, geographical and cultural backgrounds, and its recognition of such textual technicalities as variants, preferred readings, and the like. A commentary with all of the above contents should be valued as a source book for reference study, not as a substitute for original, independent study.

There are various types of Bible commentaries, each of which is geared to the particular needs of the student. A commentary may be identified under each of two classifications: (1) volume type, and (2) contents and style.

(1) Classification by Volume Type

(a) One Volume for Entire Bible

The shortest commentaries on individual books of the Bible are found in a Bible commentary which presents all sixty-six books of the Bible in the one volume. Though condensed by necessity and therefore lacking from a quantitative standpoint, this type of commentary is valuable for its identification of the *highlights* of each Bible book, easily and quickly located by the reader. Three examples of the one-volume commentary are: *Commentary on the Whole Bible*, by Robert Jamieson, A. R. Fausset, and David Brown; *The New Bible Commentary*, edited by Francis Davidson, A. M. Stibbs, and E. F. Kevan; and the more recent *Wycliffe Bible Commentary*, co-edited by Charles F. Pfeiffer and Everett F. Harrison.

(b) Individual Volume for One Bible Book.

The most common type of commentary is the individual volume on a single Bible book or a small group of books by one author. A first-rate library of commentaries would contain many works by individual authors. Each of these works should be rated high for the particular Bible book being expounded. Charles Hodge's *Commentary on the Epistle to the Romans* is one example; Merrill C. Tenney's *John: The Gospel of Belief*, written in a different style, is another.

(c) Set

Many-volumed sets of commentaries are a third type, and are valuable for their uniformity of treatment and continuity of thought from book to book. John Peter Lange's *Commentary on the Holy Scriptures* (24 volumes) is the work of many authors under one editor. The twenty-five volumes of *Biblical Commentary on the Old Testament*, by C. F. Keil and F. Delitzsch, is an example of a work by two authors. Of a highly technical nature, it is especially valuable to the advanced student in the Old Testament.

(2) Classification by Contents and Style

(a) Introductory Material

The value of a commentary is enhanced by the inclusion of a substantial amount of introductory material, such as the Bible book's authorship, date, purposes, composition, and other special studies. In building his personal library, the Bible student will usually want to choose those commentaries which give such background helps.

(b) Original Languages

Commentaries vary as to frequency of reference to the original languages. Some make no reference, though this does not necessarily imply that the author did not use the Greek or Hebrew in his study. Some commentaries make occasional reference to these languages, such as G. Campbell Morgan's very enlightening book studies. An example of the frequent use of the Greek, with a rendering of the entire

Biblical text in Greek, is F. F. Bruce's *The Acts of the Apostles*. Bruce has also written a valuable commentary on Acts for the English Bible student, *Commentary on the Book of Acts*, which is a volume of a series, *The New International Commentary on the New Testament*. For all practical purposes, a student with no Hebrew or Greek background should avoid the commentaries which give the Biblical text in only the original languages. However, he can use any of the others with real profit.

(c) Format

The format of most commentaries is verse-by-verse exegesis. This makes for easy and quick location of material, with its orderly sequential presentation. This format invites the danger, though not necessarily so, of neglecting to keep the broader relations of the text before the reader. William R. Newell's verse-by-verse commentaries very adequately aid the student to recognize such structural relations in a Bible book while he moves from verse to verse (see especially his commentary, *Romans Verse by Verse*).

G. Campbell Morgan's book studies follow a different pattern. For example, his commentary, *The Gospel According to Mark*, is divided into chapters, each devoted to a segment or passage of Scripture. Within the chapter Morgan works from paragraph to paragraph in the Biblical text, and develops a theme throughout the passage. His method parallels very closely the segment study method described in these pages.

III. PRELIMINARY BOOK SURVEY STUDY (SURVEY METHOD)

A theoretically pure inductive method would begin strictly with the smaller parts and arrive at the whole. Without doing jeopardy to the aims of the inductive approach, a preliminary survey of the *whole Biblical book* in which the segment of study lies should be made before the finer analytical studies are commenced, in order that the student may gain perspective and a fair orientation to the surrounding context. This is in keeping with Robert Browning's good advice, "Image the whole; then execute the parts." For his expository method, G. Campbell Morgan says that the four fundamental processes, in this order, are: Survey, Condensation, Expansion, and Dissection.[44] Martin Luther's approach was the same. He said he studied the Bible in the manner in which he gathered apples.[45] First, he would shake the whole tree, to let the ripest fruit fall (study of entire Bible as a unit). Then he would climb the tree and shake each limb (book survey). Then he would move to the branch, as on each limb of the tree (chapter study). Next he would shake each twig (paragraph and sentence study). Finally, he would look under each leaf (word study).

Actually, the survey suggested in these pages has all the objectivity of the inductive method, without its analytical quality.

A. Independent Study

The student's own survey is the best starting point for an analytical study. James M. Gray, who pioneered in the developing and teaching of the book survey method of study, maintained rightly that one's own original and independent study of the broad pattern of a book in the Bible, imperfect as the conclusions may be, is of far more value to the student than the most perfect outline obtained from someone else. This is not to minimize the work of others, but to emphasize that recourse to outside aids should be made only *after* the student has taken his own skyscraper view.

[44]Don M. Wagner, *The Expository Method of G. Campbell Morgan* (Westwood, N.J.: Fleming H. Revell Co., 1957), p. 50.
[45]*Die Martin Luther's Werke, Kritische Gesamtausgabe*, Vol. 2 (Weimar: H. Bohlaus Nachfolger), pp. 244-245.

1. Cursory Reading

First, read the book through at one sitting, not slowly, aloud if possible. After this reading, ask such questions as:

What are the general impressions of the book?
What atmosphere is dominant?
What key words and phrases stand out?

2. Subsequent Readings

a. Record of Observations

The book of the Bible should be read at least once more, not as quickly as the first reading, and yet not too slowly. At this stage of the survey it is wise to record any observations made along the way. One valuable survey step is the assigning of a *chapter title* to each chapter. These chapter titles are not intended to represent a logical outline of the book. Rather, the sum of them constitutes a condensed picture of the general flow of the message of the book.[46] The characteristics of a good title are:

(1) preferably one word, not more than three.
(2) picturesque words (e.g., the word "vine" instead of "union").
(3) words taken directly from the text, not a paraphrase.
(4) words which have not been used as chapter titles previously.
(5) words which tell you where you are in the book.

In the case of shorter books of the Bible, involving, say, less than six chapters, the survey can still be of a cursory quality by assigning titles to all the *paragraphs* of the book. As is noted below, the aforementioned characteristics of a chapter title apply equally well to paragraph titles.

[46] Actually, some chapter divisions do not represent accurate divisions of thought. During this preliminary survey, however, the student need not be overly concerned about adjusting any such divisions.

Because the chapter titles are not intended to represent any logical outline of the book, it is possible that the student may not have reason to make minute reference to this group of titles as a whole later in his study. Much of the value of assigning such chapter titles terminates in the actual assigning itself—it is simply another way of seeing the whole from a distant vantage point, without pressing for comprehensiveness.

Before leaving this phase of the independent survey study, the major divisions and topics of the book should be sought and identified. A good starting point is to look for any double spaces between chapters in the American Standard Version. These are usually well chosen by the editors, representing the larger divisions of thought in the book. For instance, the six chapters of Ephesians represent two major types of content: chapters one, two, and three are mainly doctrinal, whereas chapters four, five, and six are mainly practical. Stated topically, the first half teaches "What We Have In Christ," and the last half teaches "How We Should Walk In Christ." Further breakdown into smaller sections may be made by the student, depending on how much time he chooses to devote to this stage of the study. Some of the types of studies which may be made in books of the Bible are:

(1) historical   (5) chronological
(2) biographical   (6) logical
(3) geographical   (7) topical
(4) doctrinal   (8) key words

If the entire book is to be analyzed segment by segment, it is wise to make a rather thorough survey study as good preparation for the series of analyses.

At some time during the survey study, a theme or title for the book should be made. This, of course, should relate very definitely to the major divisional studies of the book. For instance, for Ephesians, a title could be "Our Life in Christ." This would relate to the two divisions, "Our Heritage in Christ" and "Our Walk in Christ." One's study is further enhanced by choosing from the book a "key" verse, which also would relate to the book title. Other things to look for in the book study would be repeated words and phrases, contrasts, progressions, climaxes, atmosphere, strategic centers.

b. The Horizontal Book Chart

For recording the observations and discoveries made in the course of one's study, the illustrated horizontal chart is suggested. The bold horizontal line is the major line, on which are written the segment or chapter divisions. It is drawn roughly in the middle of a horizontally-placed 8½ by 11 inch piece of paper. Below this line may be shown divisional studies, and above it in oblique form are recorded the chapter titles plus any other pertinent information. Such items as book title, key verse, repeated words, etc. may be placed wherever appropriate. The chart of Acts (p. 111) will illustrate the suggestions made above.

In the case of a pivotal point or strategic center in the text of a book of the Bible, as in Mark's Gospel, the structure may be indicated as shown on the chart of Mark, p. 112.

B. Use of Outside Aids

After you have made your own independent survey of a book of the Bible, it is useful to refer to outside helps, especially for information which the Bible book itself does not furnish so readily, if at all. You will want to be acquainted with such background material as:

1. authorship
2. date of writing
3. historical setting: Biblical and secular
4. geographical setting

ACTS: 35 YEARS of EARLY CHURCH HISTORY

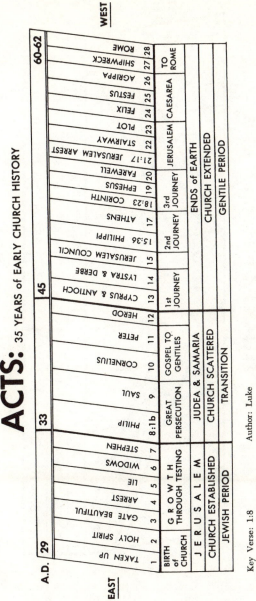

WEST — EAST

A.D. 29 | 33 | 45 | 60-62

Ch.	Event			
1	TAKEN UP	BIRTH of CHURCH	JERUSALEM	CHURCH ESTABLISHED / JEWISH PERIOD
2	HOLY SPIRIT			
3	GATE BEAUTIFUL	GROWTH THROUGH TESTING		
4	ARREST			
5	LIE			
6	WIDOWS			
7	STEPHEN			
8:1b	PHILIP	GREAT PERSECUTION	JUDEA & SAMARIA	CHURCH SCATTERED / TRANSITION
9	SAUL			
10	CORNELIUS	GOSPEL TO GENTILES		
11	PETER			
12	HEROD			
13	CYPRUS & ANTIOCH	1st JOURNEY	ENDS of EARTH	CHURCH EXTENDED / GENTILE PERIOD
14	LYSTRA & DERBE			
15	JERUSALEM COUNCIL			
15:36	PHILIPPI	2nd JOURNEY		
17	ATHENS			
18:23	CORINTH	3rd JOURNEY		
19	EPHESUS			
20	FAREWELL			
21:17	JERUSALEM ARREST		JERUSALEM	
22	STAIRWAY			
23	PLOT			
24	FELIX		CAESAREA	
25	FESTUS			
26	AGRIPPA			
27	SHIPWRECK	TO ROME		
28	ROME			

Key Verse: 1:8

Key Word: "Witness"

Author: Luke

Date Written: 61-64 A.D.

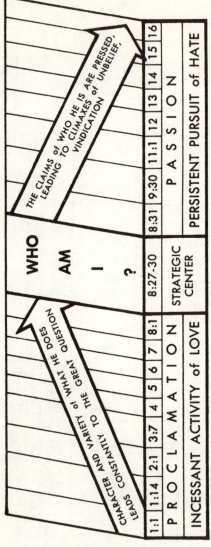

MARK: THE SERVANT JESUS

CHARACTER AND VARIETY of WHAT HE DOES CONSTANTLY LEADS TO THE GREAT QUESTION

THE CLAIMS of WHO HE IS ARE PRESSED, LEADING TO CLIMAXES of UNBELIEF, VINDICATION

WHO AM I ?

1:1	1:14	2:1	3:7	4	5	6	7	8:1	8:27-30	8:31	9:30	11:1	12	13	14	15	16
P R O C L A M A T I O N									STRATEGIC CENTER	P A S S I O N							
INCESSANT ACTIVITY of LOVE										PERSISTENT PURSUIT of HATE							

Key Verse: 10:45

Key Word: "straightway" (over 40 times)

"THE ACTIONS, NOT SO MUCH THE WORDS, of Jesus"

5. biographical setting

6. to whom or for whom the book was originally written

The more technical problems of textual criticism, higher criticism, problem passages and hermeneutical issues need not be inquired into at this point, unless the more intensive survey, as referred to above, is engaged in.

In addition to background material, the student will want to check the divisional points which he has assigned to the book of the Bible with those of other authors. Any major differences should be noted and, if necessary, adjustments made in his own outline of the book.

Outside helps, then, are intended (1) to supplement one's own study, and (2) to correct any errors of one's own study. Both the supplementary materials and the corrections should be incorporated in the horizontal book chart. It is suggested that the student record much of the background material on the back side of his horizontal chart.[47]

❀ ❀ ❀

Having taken a "skyscraper view" of the book in which smaller analytical study will be concentrated, the student is now ready to begin the more detailed analysis of a segment, recording his work on the analytical chart, the procedures of which are described in the following chapter.

[47]Note: Some students prefer to gather the background material *before* engaging in the survey procedures. This is less inductive in approach, but has the advantage which a setting can supply.

Chapter IV

CONSTRUCTION OF THE ANALYTICAL CHART

The actual construction of the analytical chart is described in these pages as comprising five basic stages.

I. STAGE ONE: PRELIMINARIES

A. Length of Segment

If the student has not already done so, he should now identify the boundaries of the segment which is to be analyzed. The segment has been arbitrarily defined as a limited group of paragraphs forming a unity. For practical purposes of study, one chapter of average length (about 25 verses)[1] is a workable segment of analytical study. The student will find that a segment of 15 to 20 verses yields the best textual re-creation study. In the case of a long chapter, it is better to study the chapter in more than one unit. For example, the long first chapter of Mark is best divided into segments represented by verses 1-13, 14-34, and 35-45. When long chapters are thus divided, one's analysis of a part of the chapter must continually be referred to the surrounding context.

[1]The following is a summary of the verse and chapter distributions in the Bible:

	Number of Verses	Number of Chapters	Average Number of Verses Per Chapter
Old Testament	23,090	929	24.8
New Testament	7,949	260	30.6
Entire Bible	31,039	1,189	26.1

Dr. Kuist, in pointing out the masterful organizational unity of Luke, chapters 1 through 9, illustrates how the so-called Infancy Narrative, following the Preface to the Gospel, is organized into segments in the American Standard Version: the annunciation of John (three paragraphs); the annunciation of Jesus (three paragraphs); the birth and naming of John (three paragraphs); the birth and naming of Jesus (three paragraphs).[2]

Some chapters, slightly longer than one considers ideal for studying by the analytical chart method, cannot properly be divided into smaller segments. Proverbs 4 with its twenty-seven verses is a good case in point. In such cases, it is better to consider the entire chapter as one segment of study and to make adjustments in the textual re-creation, as is noted below.

Appendix I gives a suggested list of study segments for six books of the Bible. The length of the segments has been kept as closely as possible to workable lengths for the analytical chart method. It is recommended that the reader refer to the opening paragraphs of this appendix at this time for further orientation.

When the student has decided upon the segment to be analyzed, he should refer to the horizontal book survey chart he has already made and notice where the segment lies in relation to the entire book. In other words, the student should identify the segment's neighbors—next door, over the back fence, and across the street—and see what it is expected to have in common with its neighbors (e.g., mainly doctrinal truth, or mainly practical truth). Is the segment at the end of a street? That is, does it conclude or begin a major section in the book? The student should be sure he knows its neighborhood, for once he enters its house for analysis, he probably won't leave the house very often during this visit.

[2]Howard T. Kuist, *These Words Upon Thy Heart*, p. 104.

B. Paragraph Divisions

If the segment of study has less than three paragraphs in the Bible version being used, one should refer to another modern version, such as the Berkeley Version, for a breakdown of the segment into at least three paragraphs. If the student still is not successful in finding smaller paragraph units, he should read the segment through a few times and attempt to make his own breakdown. Most segments of analytical chart length are divisible into at least three paragraphs, but it is wise not to force such a breakdown on the few exceptions.

Whenever new paragraph divisions are added to the segment of study, it is recommended that the student mark his Bible to indicate the extra divisions, as a visible aid in accentuating the existence of each separate paragraph. For, in structure-consciousness, one must be constantly thinking in terms of paragraphic units.

C. Paragraph Titles

Read through each paragraph and select a word or phrase (not more than three words) from the text itself, to identify the paragraph. The paragraph title should be a strong word or phrase, picturesque if possible; its only purpose is to help in identifying the paragraph it represents. It is not intended to represent part of an outline for the segment. (Refer to the discussion of chapter titles on page 108.)

D. Paragraph Themes

Look at the paragraphs again. What is each paragraph attempting to say, *generally?* How do the paragraphs differ in their general intentions? Write out on a piece of scratch paper (8½ by 11 inches) a simple theme for each paragraph so that the sum of the paragraph themes will faithfully represent the overall purpose of the whole segment. Avoid a long complex theme that is just as detailed as the paragraph itself.

Sometimes it is difficult to ascertain the main intent of a paragraph in the early stages of one's study. If the paragraph divisions are correctly placed, and the student is still having difficulty in arriving at such a paragraph theme, he might postpone this step to a later time in his study. Actually, such a situation presents one of the fascinating challenges of a structural study, namely, the discovery of the reason for the inclusion of a paragraph in the Biblical author's writing.

E. Initial Observations

Just about now the student's scratch paper becomes a busy terminal for notations about things being observed. Since there is no rhyme nor reason in the *order* of a student's observations, it is advisable to jot them down in simple list form, perhaps numbering them consecutively to give some semblance of order.

There is no set procedure as to what to look for in this stage of study. These are the first fresh moments of one's visit in the many-roomed mansion of the Scripture passage. Read to be impressed, and in passages familiar to the student from previous years he will do well to cultivate the "innocence of the eye," reading the text as though he had never seen it before. Also, he should remember that observation is the art of seeing things *as they really are.*

Some students prefer, in the initial stages of study, to answer such simple and basic questions as, Who? What? Where? When? Why? These might be called skeletal questions, and should serve with the view to being later clothed upon with the "meat" of the Word. Miles Coverdale's advice in his preface to his famous version of the English Bible of 1535 is often referred to. He wrote:

It shall greatly help thee to understand Scripture if thou
wilt mark not only what is spoken or written, but of whom
and unto whom, with what words, at what time, where, to
what intent, with what circumstances, considering what
goeth before and what followeth after.

In addition to the scratch paper on which the student is
recording observations as they are made, he will want now to
take another scratch paper (8½ by 11 inches) and begin to
make notations on a rough analytical chart. Holding the
paper vertically, the student should draw a rectangle 4 by
9 inches, centered on the page (see page 120). This represents the segment frame. Then, this frame should be divided
into as many parts as there are paragraphs in the segment,
with proportional space given to each paragraph, depending
on the number of verses contained therein. Within this segment frame nothing but the Bible text is written or printed.
The outside margins are for outlines, extra-Biblical notations,
quotes, cross-references, etc.

At the beginning of his study, the student should record
the following on this rough analytical chart:

1. the reference for the segment study, e.g., MARK 1:1-
13, placed at the very top-center of the page.

2. the reference and description of the book division in
which the segment lies, e.g.,

1:1—3:35
POPULARITY AND OPPOSITION

placed in the top right-hand corner.

3. the verse references for the beginning of each paragraph, placed in the upper left-hand corner of each *paragraph* frame. Also, the last verse of the segment is placed in
the lower left corner of the *segment* frame.

4. the paragraph title, printed in small letters in the upper
right-hand corner of each paragraph frame, and underlined.

Whatever observations are made now in the more cursory stage of study may be recorded with normal handwriting script. On the permanent analytical chart, however, it is strongly urged that the student use print, even though more time is involved in this type of recording. This writer considers this aspect of the analytical chart so vital that his own students are required to print their analyses. Actually, the time element in printing will be reduced considerably with experience.

At this point the student's worksheet will look something like that shown on the following page.

F. Setting the Goals: The Three Major Components of an Analytical Chart

The analytical chart when completed will contain many items, both general and detailed. Basically, however, it is made up of three major components:

1. *Textual Re-creation.* This is a recasting of the actual Biblical text (without additions or comments) printed within the segment frame.
2. *A Main Topical Study.* This is a major study of *one* subject within the entire segment, and is made the dominant study on the analytical chart.
3. *Supplementary Studies.* All other items, including observations, outlines, word studies, and topical studies, make up the remainder of the analytical chart.

The above three components comprise the next three stages of the analytical chart method, as they are described in the following pages. The main topical study is treated first, however, for reasons which will be apparent later. The student should indelibly fix in his mind that the items listed above are the major goals of his analytical chart. This will help in motivation and direction in the midst of detailed studies.

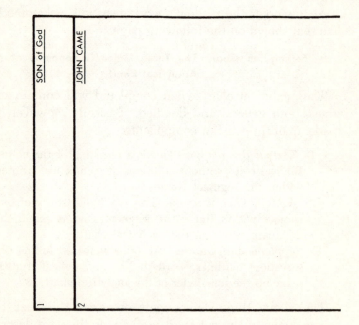

MARK 1:1-13

1:1—3:35
POPULARITY
AND
OPPOSITION

SON of God

1

JOHN CAME

2

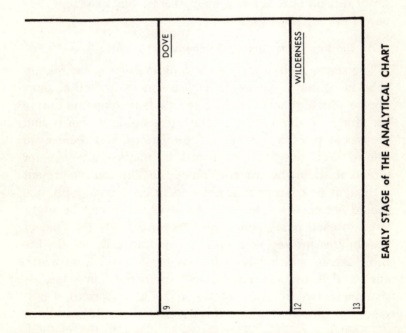

EARLY STAGE of THE ANALYTICAL CHART

II. STAGE TWO: A MAIN TOPICAL STUDY

Since the segment is a compositional unit of thought, it is the Biblical author's intention for that segment to teach or convey *one main thought,* plus other auxiliary truths. Many of the auxiliary truths are developed simultaneously in each of the paragraphs of the segment, forming therefore many segment topical studies. It should be understood that the main topical study of the analytical chart is not necessarily the Biblical author's main theme, but may represent one of the auxiliary studies.

A. The Key Center and Its Relations

The starting place for a main topical study is the finding of a key center in the segment. It is usually a word or short phrase which attaches itself to the student sometime during his study of the passage. The attractions of words and phrases as possible key centers are various, and there is no rule to direct one to a key center. In practice, a key center directs itself to the student. Since this key must represent a thought or concept that is found in each paragraph, one should not choose a word or phrase which cannot be so related to each paragraph. This of course limits the field of possibilities for key centers, but not drastically so. In the Bible classes which this writer has taught, and from which analytical charts are received as part of the homework assignments, twenty-five analyses of the same Scriptural passage will usually render an average of about twenty-three different key centers. This serves to illustrate the plethora of interweaving of truths from paragraph to paragraph within a study segment.

In choosing the key center, be sure that it relates to another phrase within the paragraph in which the key center is found, in addition to each other paragraph. Also, the key center should relate to a *different* aspect of some common truth, in each paragraph. For example, if a key center reads "JESUS CAME," and this relates to the thought, "JESUS CAME TO MEN IN DARKNESS" in one paragraph, it should not be made to relate to a *similar* thought in another paragraph, at least for this main topical study.

For purposes of clarity, it is recommended that the key center be made to relate to only *one* truth for each paragraph, if the segment constitutes more than two paragraphs. The relations which it bears to any additional thoughts within the paragraph may be indicated in the margin of the analytical chart, as subpoints under each main paragraphic point (see below). For segments of study which contain only two paragraphs, it is generally wise to refer the key center to at least two unrepeated truths within each paragraph, in order to give substantial range to this topical study.

B. Recording This Study

1. *In the Bible*

Since the Biblical text will be recast and recorded in the segment frame on the analytical chart, it is advisable to mark in one's Bible the key center and the one phrase of each paragraph to which it is related, so that these phrases may appear to be predominant when it comes time to record the textual re-creation (Stage Three).

2. *On a Rough Worksheet*

Before recording the main topical study on the permanent analytical chart, write out this part of the study on a scratch worksheet containing the segment frame. Four things are involved here:

a. Record the key center in its approximate location in the paragraph frame. Every word in the key center is taken from the Biblical text, and the entire phrase should be as short as possible without destroying the clarity of the truth intended. If words within a phrase are omitted in order to emphasize the surrounding words, the omission should be indicated by three dots, as "THE SPIRIT DRIVETH ... INTO THE WILDERNESS" (Mark 1:12) (use four dots if a period is also omitted). On the permanent analytical chart the key center is printed as the largest or most outstanding phrase in the study. (Refer to the chart on page 128.)

b. In each paragraph frame, including the paragraph in which the key center is located, write the phrase to which the key center is being related. Again, for clarity's sake, the number of words in the phrase should be kept to a minimum, still showing the relation.

c. Construct a *master title* for this main topical study, and record it at the top of the segment frame, just under the passage reference. This title usually represents one's own wording, though it may be identical to the key center. This wording should relate specifically to the key center. In order to assure this specific relation, it is best to include in the title at least one of the strong words in the key center. For the key center "THE SPIRIT DRIVETH . . . INTO THE WILDERNESS," a title such as "EXPERIENCES OF JESUS" does not *specifically* relate to the key center, though it surely relates in a general way. A correct title might be, "WILDERNESS LESSONS," the inclusion of the word "wilderness" assuring this specific relation.

d. *Secure paragraph points* for this topical study, and record them in bold print in the left-hand margin of the analytical chart, opposite the phrase already recorded in each paragraph. The paragraph points must relate *in thought* to the Biblical phrases in the paragraphs, and they must also relate *in thought* and *gram-*

matically to the master title. Consider as an example the segment MARK 1:1-13, involving the four paragraphs, namely, verses 1; 2-8; 9-11; and 12-13. A key center could be "JESUS CAME" (verse 9); the master title could be identical with the key center, i.e., "JESUS CAME." The four paragraph points and their Biblical references, respectively, might be worded thus:

Paragraph Point	*Biblical Text*
1. Bringing Good Tidings	"gospel" (1)
2. As Announced By John	"There cometh after me he . . . mightier than I" (7)
3. With the Blessing of His Father	"Thou art my beloved Son" (11)
4. To Be Driven Into the Wilderness	"The Spirit driveth him forth into the wilderness" (12)

These paragraph points have been worded so that they will relate in thought and in grammatical construction to the master title. The test for this grammatical relation is to state the master title before each paragraph point, thus:

Master Title	*Paragraph Point*
Jesus Came.	Bringing Good Tidings
Jesus Came.	As Announced by John
Jesus Came.	With the Blessing of His Father
Jesus Came.	To be Driven Into the Wilderness

To the homiletician or preacher it will be obvious at this point that the above topical study involves the elements basic to expository preaching. This is one of the further practical aspects of the analytical chart method, which will be referred to later.

At this point, the student's rough analytical chart will look something like that on pages 128 and 129.

The student may choose now to transfer this same material to the permanent analytical chart, unless he feels that he wants to do more experimentation with the wording of the master title and paragraph points, and the like, in which case it would be better to postpone recording the marginal studies. In either case, if at this point the student chooses to record permanently his studies involving the *Biblical text itself* within the segment frame, he should be sure that in his printing of the key center and paragraph phrases, all of which appear within this segment frame, he leaves enough space for the remainder of the Biblical text of each paragraph. With experience he will learn to estimate rather accurately how much space on an analytical chart the printing of the Biblical text requires.

III. STAGE THREE: TEXTUAL RE-CREATION

One of the crucial phases of the analytical chart method is the re-creation of the Biblical text. The wise student will apply himself conscientiously to develop this skill. On the analytical chart the re-created text is recorded within the segment frame. As was stated above, only the Biblical text appears within this segment frame.

A. The Meaning and Purpose of Textual Re-creation

A comparison of the printed Bible text and a re-created text will serve to describe what textual re-creation is. (See page 131). The printed text in your Bible runs from margin to margin and, except for italicized words which represent words not in the Biblical manuscripts, the print is very uniform. The small letter, without embellishments, is the common type of print used, except for beginnings of sentences, for proper names, or for occasional entire words (e.g., LORD), when capital letters are used. Indentations are seldom used for anything other than the beginning of new paragraphs, for quotations of Scripture, or for the usual poetical structure. In other words, the format of the printed text in the Bible is rather homogeneous.

In textual re-creation, on the other hand, various graphic devices are used to indicate the actual grammatical and thought structure of a Scriptural passage. Such structure involves relations of words to words, relations of clauses to clauses, cores of sentences, distinctions between primary and subordinate phrases, listings of items, laws of composition, and many other structural items.

The purpose of textual re-creation is to *pictorialize* the Biblical text so that it is made to speak for itself without the intrusion of comment from outside. By so recasting the text in thought pattern, without omitting, adding or altering anything of the text, new and wide vistas are opened to the student's eye in his observations. The re-created text becomes the basic framework about which all other studies are made.

B. How to Record Textual Re-creation

As stated above, various graphic devices are used to show the many relations within a text. If only one such device were used, the result would be homogeneity in one of two extremes: confusion or fusion. For textual re-creation, therefore, *various* graphic aids should be used such as:

indentations	various colors
underlinings	arrows
large and small capitalizations	numerical listings
small-type letters	blank spaces
circling, boxing	color shading

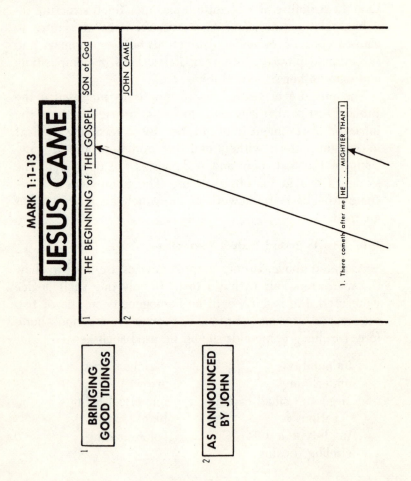

MARK 1:1-13

JESUS CAME

THE BEGINNING of THE GOSPEL

SON of God

1   JOHN CAME

1. There cometh after me HE ... MIGHTIER THAN I

1:1—3:35
POPULARITY
AND
OPPOSITION

1
BRINGING
GOOD TIDINGS

2
AS ANNOUNCED
BY JOHN

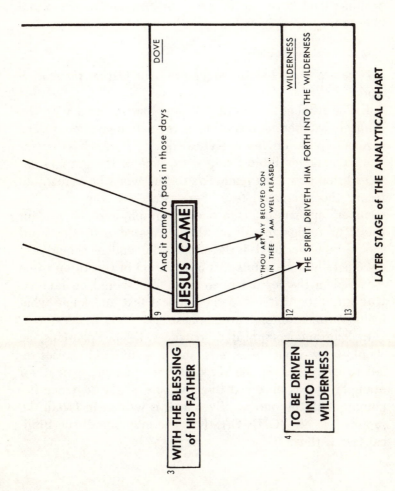

DOVE

And it came to pass in those days

JESUS CAME

"THOU ART MY BELOVED SON
IN THEE I AM WELL PLEASED."

WILDERNESS

THE SPIRIT DRIVETH HIM FORTH INTO THE WILDERNESS

9

12

13

LATER STAGE of THE ANALYTICAL CHART

3 WITH THE BLESSING
of HIS FATHER

4 TO BE DRIVEN
INTO THE
WILDERNESS

There is no one standard procedure in re-creating the text. The best way to learn this step is by doing. On the following page an example of a textual re-creation of Mark 1:2-8 is shown, for purposes of comparison, below the Biblical text which it recasts. The device of color, of course, cannot be shown here. (Normally, most of the re-created text is printed in one standard color of ink, e.g., black. For emphases, some words and phrases are printed in other colors, or underlined or circled in color. Further, some arrows and lines are made in color.)

C. Helpful Suggestions

Here are some helpful suggestions for textual re-creation work:

1. The student should be fairly well acquainted with the Biblical text before recording a textual re-creation in the segment frame on the analytical chart. It is advisable for him to mark his Bible freely with some of the graphic devices listed above, as reminders to him when he is ready to record the re-created text. For instance, if the word "remember" appears often in one paragraph, and the student wants to recognize this in the re-created text, the word should be underlined in the Bible. The student should also anticipate how he wants this observation of repetition to be recorded in the textual re-creation. He should be familiar with any lists of items in the Biblical text and know what main words he intends to emphasize.

In long and complicated sentences, as in Ephesians, he should know what the core is, and how different clauses relate to each other. In the Mark 1:2-8 re-creation segment, for example, it was observed that the core of the sentence beginning with the phrase, "Even as it is written in Isaiah the prophet . . ." is "JOHN CAME." The intention of the Biblical text is thus:

MARK 1:2-8

2 Even as it is written in Isaiah the prophet, Behold, I send my messenger before thy face, Who shall prepare thy way; 3 The voice of one crying in the wilderness, Make ye ready the way of the Lord, Make his paths straight; 4 John came, who baptized in the wilderness and preached the baptism of repentance unto remission of sins. 5 And there went out unto him all the country of Judaea, and all they of Jerusalem; and they were baptized of him in the river Jordan, confessing their sins. 6 And John was clothed with camel's hair, and had a leathern girdle about his loins, and did eat locusts and wild honey. 7 And he preached, saying, There cometh after me he that is mightier than I, the latchet of whose shoes I am not worthy to stoop down and unloose. 8 I baptized you in water; but he shall baptize you in the Holy Spirit. (A.S.V.)

MARK 1:2-8

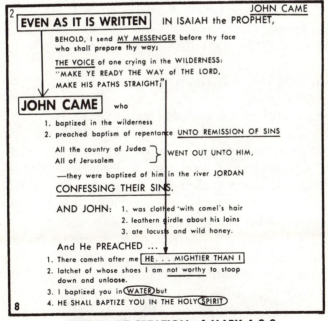

TEXTUAL RE-CREATION of MARK 1:2-8

"Even as it is written"—the Prophecy
"John came"—the Fulfillment

So, in recasting this Biblical text, these two parts of the extended sentence are shown to be related to each other by drawing a line, and since the dual truth of prophecy and fulfillment in John has a close affinity with the key center which had been chosen, "JESUS CAME," it was anticipated to emphasize this in the segment frame when the time came for printing the textual re-creation.

2. While fair familiarity with the text should precede the actual recording of the textual re-creation, the student should not hesitate to do the actual recording because he feels he has not *exhausted* his observations on the text. After he has recorded the textual re-creation, he will begin to see new things which he had not seen until the text was recast in print. This illustrates one of the major values of textual re-creation: It opens one's eyes to greater discoveries in the text.

3. During the early stages of learning this study process, it is advisable to sketch roughly on scratch paper the textual re-creation before it is recorded on the permanent analytical chart. The reason is obvious. Actually, adequate skill in textual re-creation comes rather quickly to the average student. Whatever time is spent and patience exerted in learning will be amply rewarded. To be sure, the mental skill of recasting the thought pattern of a Bible passage is worth more than gold to the Bible exegete.

4. When the text is printed in the paragraph frame the normal *general* pattern of movement from top to bottom should be followed rather than making the text jump around in a labyrinthine fashion.

5. The student should avoid the pitfall of setting down isolated groups of text within the paragraph frame. The

entire paragraphic text in its re-created form should reveal a "togetherness" from start to finish.

6. To overdo any one graphic device will usually result in confusion. The student can avoid this by using as many graphic devices as possible.

7. No significant phrase in the Biblical text should be left out unless the omission is indicated in the re-created text by three or four dots.

8. The re-created text should be proportionately distributed in the paragraph frame. While the student is doing the recording, he ought to check himself from time to time. For instance, when he is midway in the paragraph in the Bible, he should be approximately midway in the paragraph frame. For long segments, smaller printing and more of the allowable omissions are necessary. It is for such segments that fine-line pens and pencils will be useful or necessary.

9. The main topical study (Stage Two) should be the predominant part of an analytical chart. This means that within the segment frame the key center should stand shoulder-high above all other parts of the textual re-creation.

10. Good textual re-creation provides accurate emphases and allows for nothing which will jeopardize clarity. It goes without saying that any textual re-creation which is less accurate or less clear than the Biblical text itself defeats its own purpose.

IV. STAGE FOUR: SUPPLEMENTARY STUDIES

After incorporating both the textual re-creation and the main topical study on the permanent chart, the student is ready to record other observations on the chart. Some of those observations have already been made. Many of them are yet to be made. Since all that is recorded hereafter must be placed in the margins, space is at a premium. Therefore, whatever related studies are recorded should be worded as succinctly and briefly as possible. Long comments or quotations should be reserved for the back side of the chart, referred to by a cross-reference. See pages 138 and 139 for the marginal notations on the Mark 1:1-13 analytical chart.

Supplementary studies involve anything in the text of the segment. They may be further detailed studies on the main topical study of Stage Two, though most of them are not so related.

A. Varieties of Studies, and How to Record Them

Basically, there are two main types of textual studies. One is the *isolated* type, which has reference to *one* particular word or phrase or structure of the text, without relating it particularly to anything else in the segment. Word studies comprise a large percentage of the isolated type of study, the source of which is often an outside help, such as a commentary. For instance, it is pointed out by at least one commentary that the word "driveth" in the phrase "The Spirit driveth him forth into the wilderness" (Mark 1:12) is the same Greek word used to describe the violent action when Jesus "cast out" demons. This is an isolated type of observation. See chart of Mark 1:1-13 (p. 138).

The second type of textual study is the *related* type. Any observation which refers to *more than one* item in the text is of this type. In the sample analytical chart of Mark 1:1-13 the right-hand margin records the following comparison, of the related type:

Prophets' Prophecy of John
—Fulfillment

John's Prophecy of Jesus
—Fulfillment

The related type of study may indicate comparison, contrast, progression, or simple summation of items. The study may be confined to one paragraph, or to more than one paragraph. The most interesting type of related study is perhaps that which involves the consecutive study of a word or topic through *all* the paragraphs of the segment. Many times interesting laws of composition are discovered here, such as climax, or interchange. For his independent study, the student is encouraged to concentrate his looking on such *related* studies and postpone much of the isolated-type looking to later recourse to outside helps, which by their very nature usually offer that kind of help. Also, the student should not succumb to the temptation to write a comment in the margins for every isolated truth in the text. For one thing, marginal spaces do not have large accommodations and, secondly, the average student does not need as much training in the isolated-type observation as in the related type. This need was illustrated earlier in Chapter II where it was remarked that much present-day so-called expository preaching is really only verse-by-verse detached commentary.

Examples of the related type of study will be given below. There are many varieties of studies, related or isolated, which the student will record on his analytical chart. The following list suggests some of these possibilities.

1. Context, Before and After

In order to show how the segment is related to what goes before, an arrow should be drawn from the top left-hand corner of the segment frame obliquely into the top of the page, and the relation, such as *cause-effect*, should be stated specifically. One of the opening words or phrases in the first paragraph may be the transitional connector between the previous segment and the one now being studied. In such a case an arrow should be drawn from these words or phrases. To show how the entire segment or the last paragraph is related to what follows, the arrow should extend from the bottom line of the segment, or from a word or phrase within the last paragraph, toward the bottom of the page.

Examples:

MARK 3:7-19a (p. 144). The title "Why They Came to Jesus" is related to the previous segment (2:18–3:6) by way of contrast, the previous segment showing why they OPPOSED Jesus. As seen on the chart, the relating device is an arrow.

MARK 1:1-13 (p. 138). The last paragraph, which teaches Jesus' *proving* for the ministry, is shown to relate to what immediately follows in Mark, where Mark deals with the *ministry itself* (14ff): Jesus preached (14), called (17), taught (21), healed (26).

2. *General Paragraph Content*

It is wise to distinguish the different parts of a segment early in the analytical study. If the segment is narrative writing, how much of it is action? How much is speech or conversation? How much is editorial comment? If the segment is generally doctrinal, as in the epistles, how much is factual? How much is command or exhortation? How much is warning? If there is a time pattern in the segment, how much is past? Present? Future? One recurrent pattern in the Bible, especially in historical sections, is that of cause and effect. Three paragraphs in a segment of Acts, for example, may present cause, effect, and sequel, respectively. These and other broad thought structures of a Bible passage should be recognized in the earlier stages of one's study. These structures may be recorded on the chart by printing the appropriate descriptive words in the margin at the respective location. Or, a vertical space may be constructed by drawing a vertical line approximately one-quarter inch wide parallel to and adjoining one of the vertical lines of the segment frame (see sample chart of Mark 3:7-19a). The descriptive words may be printed in these spaces.

Examples:

MARK 1:1-13 (p. 138). The second, third, and fourth paragraphs show Jesus as the *object* of action. In the second paragraph He is preached about; in the third He is baptized and anointed; in the fourth He is tempted. This is quite a contrast to the very next passage in Mark, where Jesus is shown to be the *actor*, preaching, calling, and teaching.

MARK 3:7-19a (p. 144). The first paragraph has an atmosphere of activity and violence, and the second has an atmosphere of quietness and deliberation. In the first paragraph Jesus is dealing with multitudes; in the last He is dealing with individuals. The activity, violence, and multitudes of the first paragraph are borne out also by the marginal study recorded thus: much people; much greatness; much healing; much press; much noise; much charge.

3. *Word and Topical Studies*

One of the more frequent studies made in a Scripture passage is the related-type word study. If there is an oft repeated word in the passage, this repetition may be recorded either by underlining the word as it appears in each paragraph, or printing it unobtrusively in the margin for each occurrence in the segment. See the final-stage chart of Romans 8:26-39 (p. 154) for the appearances of the phrase "all things," as recorded in the left-hand margin. A study of contrasting or similar words or phrases may also be so indicated.

The study of a topic throughout a segment, a fascinating experience for the student, is not always an easy type of study. Such topical studies, which are similar to the main topical study already made, are intended to supplement one's analysis of the passage in the area of related studies. For

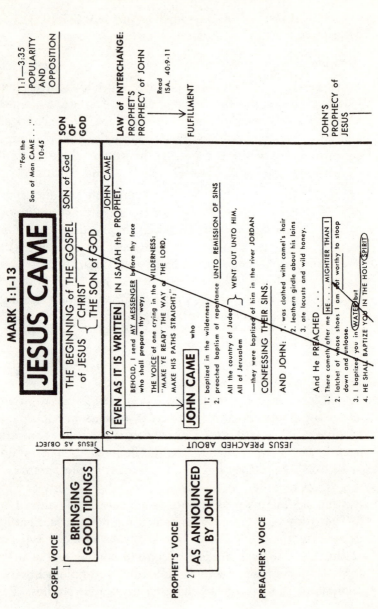

MARK 1:1-13

JESUS CAME

"For the Son of Man CAME . . . ." 10:45

THE BEGINNING of THE GOSPEL
of JESUS { CHRIST
          THE SON of GOD

SON of God   SON OF GOD

1:1—3:35
POPULARITY
AND
OPPOSITION

EVEN AS IT IS WRITTEN   IN ISAIAH the PROPHET,

LAW of INTERCHANGE:
PROPHET'S
PROPHECY of JOHN

Read
ISA. 40:9-11

BEHOLD, I send MY MESSENGER before thy face
who shall prepare thy way;

THE VOICE of one crying in the WILDERNESS:
"MAKE YE READY THE WAY of THE LORD,
MAKE HIS PATHS STRAIGHT,"

JOHN CAME

JOHN CAME   who

FULFILLMENT

1. baptized in the wilderness
2. preached baptism of repentance UNTO REMISSION OF SINS

All the country of Judea } WENT OUT UNTO HIM,
All of Jerusalem

—they were baptized of him in the river JORDAN
CONFESSING THEIR SINS.

AND JOHN: 1. was clothed with camel's hair
            2. leathern girdle about his loins
            3. ate locusts and wild honey.

And He PREACHED . . . .

1. There cometh after me [HE . . . . MIGHTIER THAN I]

2. latchet of whose shoes I am not worthy to stoop
   down and unloose.

3. I baptized you in WATER but

4. HE SHALL BAPTIZE YOU IN THE HOLY SPIRIT

JOHN'S
PROPHECY of
JESUS

JESUS AS OBJECT   JESUS PREACHED ABOUT

GOSPEL VOICE

1 BRINGING
GOOD TIDINGS

PROPHET'S VOICE

2 AS ANNOUNCED
BY JOHN

PREACHER'S VOICE

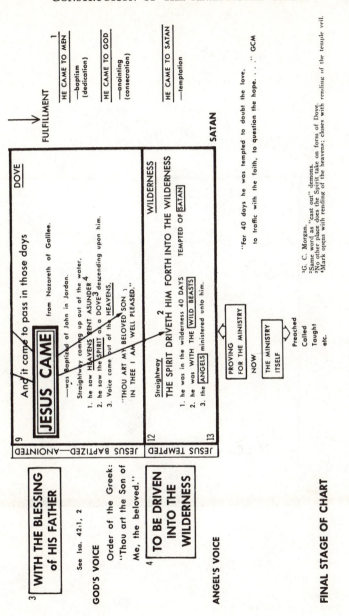

FULFILLMENT

HE CAME TO MEN
—baptism (dedication)

HE CAME TO GOD
—anointing (consecration)

HE CAME TO SATAN
—temptation

DOVE

And it came to pass in those days

JESUS CAME   from Nazareth of Galilee.

—was Baptized of John in Jordan.

Straightway coming up out of the water,

1. he saw HEAVENS RENT ASUNDER [4]
2. he saw the SPIRIT of a DOVE [3] descending upon him.
3. Voice came out of the HEAVENS,

"THOU ART MY BELOVED SON [1]
IN THEE I AM WELL PLEASED."

WILDERNESS

Straightway [2]
THE SPIRIT DRIVETH HIM FORTH INTO THE WILDERNESS   TEMPTED OF SATAN

1. he was in the wilderness 40 DAYS
2. he was WITH THE WILD BEASTS
3. the ANGELS ministered unto him.

JESUS BAPTIZED—ANOINTED

JESUS TEMPTED

3 WITH THE BLESSING of HIS FATHER

See Isa. 42:1, 2

GOD'S VOICE

Order of the Greek:
"Thou art the Son of Me, the beloved."

4 TO BE DRIVEN INTO THE WILDERNESS

ANGEL'S VOICE

SATAN

"For 40 days he was tempted to doubt the love,
to traffic with the faith, to question the hope. . . ." GCM

PROVING FOR THE MINISTRY

NOW

THE MINISTRY ITSELF

Preached
Called
Taught
etc.

[1] G. C. Morgan.
[2] Same word as "cast out" demons.
[3] No other place does the Spirit take on form of Dove.
[4] Mark opens with rending of the heavens; closes with rending of the temple veil.

FINAL STAGE OF CHART

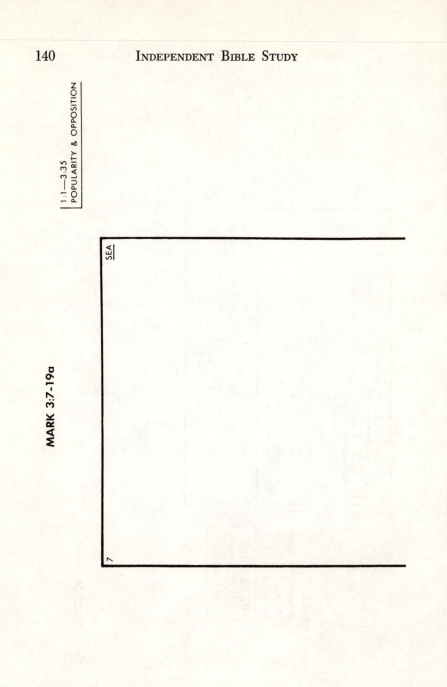

1:1—3:35
POPULARITY & OPPOSITION

MARK 3:7-19a

SEA

7

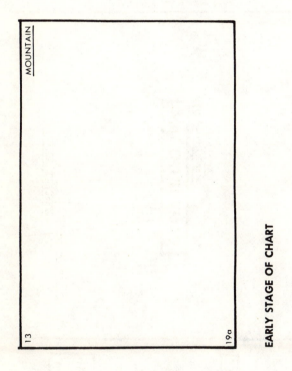

MOUNTAIN

13

19a

EARLY STAGE OF CHART

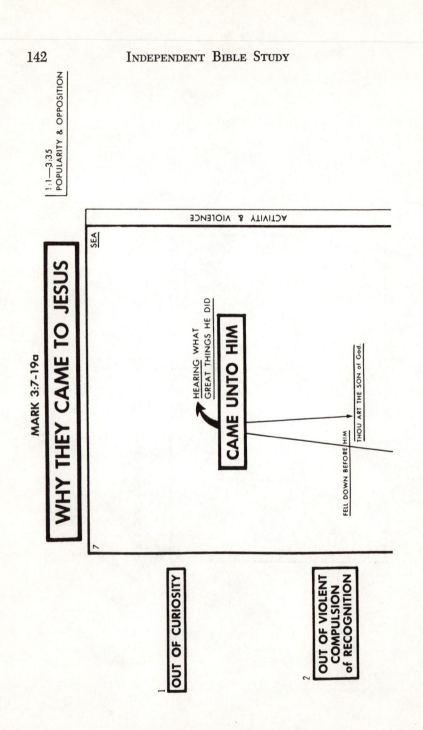

MARK 3:7-19a

WHY THEY CAME TO JESUS

1:1—3:35
POPULARITY & OPPOSITION

ACTIVITY & VIOLENCE

SEA

CAME UNTO HIM

HEARING WHAT GREAT THINGS HE DID

FELL DOWN BEFORE HIM

THOU ART THE SON of God.

1 OUT OF CURIOSITY

2 OUT OF VIOLENT COMPULSION of RECOGNITION

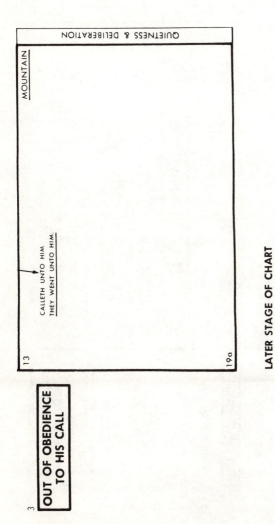

LATER STAGE OF CHART

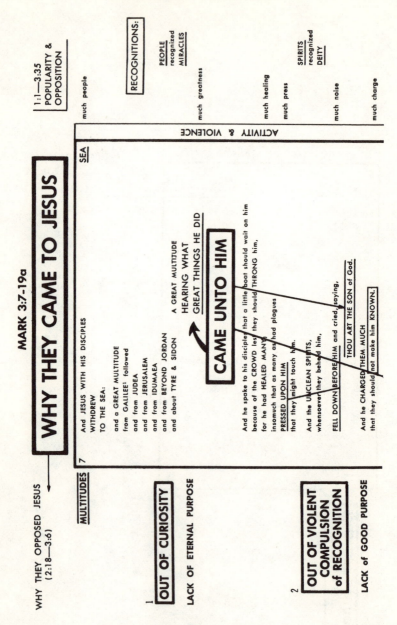

MARK 3:7-19a

WHY THEY OPPOSED JESUS
(2:18—3:6)

WHY THEY CAME TO JESUS

1:1—3:35
POPULARITY &
OPPOSITION

RECOGNITIONS:

PEOPLE
recognized
MIRACLES

much people

much greatness

much healing

much press

SPIRITS
recognized
DEITY

much noise

much charge

ACTIVITY & VIOLENCE

SEA

MULTITUDES 7

And JESUS WITH HIS DISCIPLES
WITHDREW
TO THE SEA:

and a GREAT MULTITUDE
from GALILEE¹ followed
and from JUDEA
and from JERUSALEM
and from IDUMAEA
and from BEYOND JORDAN
and about TYRE & SIDON

A GREAT MULTITUDE
HEARING WHAT
GREAT THINGS HE DID

CAME UNTO HIM

And he spoke to his disciple that a little boat should wait on him
because of the CROWD lest they should THRONG him,
for he had HEALED MANY;
insomuch that as many as had plagues
PRESSED UPON HIM
that they might touch him.

And the UNCLEAN SPIRITS,
whensoever they beheld him,

FELL DOWN BEFORE HIM and cried, saying,
THOU ART THE SON of God.

And he CHARGED THEM MUCH
that they should not make him KNOWN.

1
OUT OF CURIOSITY
LACK of ETERNAL PURPOSE

2
**OUT OF VIOLENT
COMPULSION
of RECOGNITION**
LACK of GOOD PURPOSE

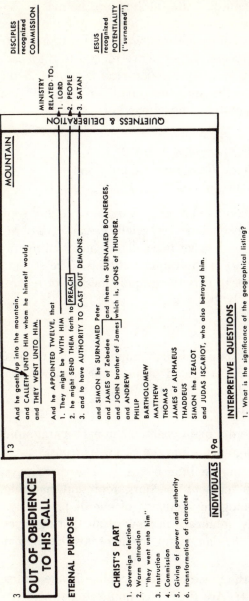

OUT OF OBEDIENCE TO HIS CALL

ETERNAL PURPOSE

CHRIST'S PART

1. Sovereign election
2. Warm attraction "they went unto him"
3. Instruction
4. Commission
5. Giving of power and authority
6. transformation of character

__INDIVIDUALS__

13 MOUNTAIN

And he goeth up into the mountain,
and CALLETH UNTO HIM whom he himself would;
and THEY WENT UNTO HIM.

And he APPOINTED TWELVE, that
1. They might be WITH HIM
2. he might SEND THEM forth to [PREACH]
3. and to have AUTHORITY TO CAST OUT DEMONS.

and SIMON he SURNAMED Peter
and JAMES of Zebedee ⎤ and them he SURNAMED BOANERGES,
and JOHN brother of James ⎦ which is, SONS of THUNDER.
and ANDREW
PHILIP
BARTHOLOMEW
MATTHEW
THOMAS
JAMES of ALPHAEUS
THADDEUS
SIMON the ZEALOT
and JUDAS ISCARIOT, who also betrayed him.

19a

QUIETNESS & DELIBERATION

MINISTRY RELATED TO:
1. LORD
2. PEOPLE
3. SATAN

DISCIPLES recognized COMMISSION

JESUS recognized POTENTIALITY ("surnamed")

INTERPRETIVE QUESTIONS

1. What is the significance of the geographical listing?
2. Why did the unclean spirits give this confession?
   Why did Jesus give such a charge?
3. WHAT IS the significance of the 3-fold commission to the twelve? Why twelve?
4. Why the surnaming?

†Note the omission of Samaria from the list.

FINAL STAGE OF CHART

recording a topical study, write the topic in the margin opposite the top of the segment frame, use any graphic device to identify it as a heading, and below it, in the appropriate marginal positions, record the sequence related to the heading. For example, a study of RECOGNITION is shown in the right-hand margin of the analytical chart for Mark 3:7-19a (p. 144). The consecutive points are:

> *People Recognize Miracles*
> *The Spirits Recognize Deity*
> *The Disciples Recognize Commission*
> *Jesus Recognizes Potentiality*

The student is encouraged to make various word and topical studies as described above, especially because they are of the related type and serve to lead one more intimately to the overall purposes of the Biblical authors. The student should also remember to vary the graphic method of recording each study, for clarity's sake.

4. Setting

One of the more simple though important observations concerns local setting. Such an observation is more common in the historical sections of the Bible. Make small notations in the margin on such items as:

a. PERSONS. Is there a main character in each paragraph? Look for any significance in the cast of persons.

b. TIME. Watch for the time element. The three paragraphs of one segment in Mark represent morning, noon, and evening, respectively, of one of Jesus' days, and this fact is significant in view of all that occurred in each part of the day, taxing to the utmost His human strength.

c. PLACES. Does the place of action change in the course of one segment? Are there any implications?

d. Events. Look for any pattern in the sequence of events, such as sermon; reaction; explanation—a sequence occurring more than once in the Acts of the Apostles.

Whether or not any significant sequence or pattern is detected in the setting of a passage, it is generally wise to record the basic elements of the setting somewhere on the analytical chart. Many times the intersection of such basic data can be more significant than one would anticipate. In the recording of the observation, unless the particular fact is of major importance, it should not be made to stand out above other more important studies.

5. *Laws of Composition*

The observation of a law of composition, such as interchange or cruciality, is obviously not an end in itself. Yet it is recommended that the student identify on his analytical chart any such law which appears to him to be significant. Actually, because words and phrases are involved in the compositional structure of the passage, this study is a type of word or topical study; and, because of the compositional law involved, it is usually a very intriguing study. Refer to Chapter II for a description of the various laws of composition, and be on the lookout for such laws in the Scripture passage.

Example:

Mark 1:1-13 (p. 138). The law of interchange is illustrated by the beautiful way in which Mark relates John's coming to Jesus' coming. The sequence runs thus:

> A. The Prophets' Prophecy of John
> B. The Fulfillment
> A. John's Prophecy of Jesus
> B. The Fulfillment

6. *Atmosphere*

What is the atmosphere of the segment as a whole? Suppose it were treachery and hate. Then write these words toward the top of one of the margins. If each paragraph betrays differing atmospheres, record accordingly. As has already been pointed out, the identification of atmosphere is a helpful clue in one's interpretation of a passage.

Example:

MARK 3:7-19a (p. 144). As noted above, the first paragraph is shown to have an atmosphere of activity and violence, while the second paragraph betrays quietness and deliberation.

7. *Comparison of Beginning and End*

If a book does not "go anywhere" or "do anything" between its first chapter and last, there is question as to its reason for existing. Because so much of eternal significance happens between Genesis and Revelation, the Bible stands as a giant among books. When studying a short passage within one of the books of the Bible, such as a segment, it is always an interesting experience to compare the first verse(s) of that segment with the last verse(s). The student should use his ingenuity as to how to record any such observation. For example, Mark 1:1-13 goes from good tidings to wilderness, from the Son of God to Satan, the supposedly dark ending of the last paragraph being interpreted by the victory note of the first.

8. *Amplification of Paragraph Points*

For each of the paragraph points which have been recorded in connection with the main topical study, the student may desire to make a more detailed study of each such paragraph point, for purposes of explanation. The logical place for recording such subpoints would be under each paragraph point.

Example:

ROMANS 8:26-39. Notice the amplifications under the paragraph points (p. 154).

9. *Relation of a Passage to the Entire Book*

If the theme of the whole book is kept in mind during one's analysis of a smaller passage, the student may notice a relation between the two which he wishes to recognize. For example, the key center of Mark, "Who Am I?" (Mark 8:27-30) will be continually referred to in reference to Christ's identity in various study passages. Do not overdo this and, at the same time, do not overlook it.

Another type of relation reference is illustrated by the phrase appearing early in Mark's Gospel, "he saw the heavens rent asunder" (Mark 1:10), which is related to a phrase appearing at the end of the Gospel, "And the veil of the temple was rent in two. . . ." (Mark 15:38). This observation is recorded on the Mark 1:1-13 analytical chart by the device of this footnote (p. 139):

Mark *opens* with the RENDING OF THE HEAVENS (1:10)

Mark *closes* with the RENDING OF THE TEMPLE VEIL (15:38)

This notation also illustrates the use of footnotes in the bottom marginal space. It is recommended that at least the left half of the bottom margin be reserved for footnotes.

B. Recording Outside Helps

When the student comes to the later stages in his study and begins to refer to commentaries, word studies, and other helps, he will come across those things which he will want to incorporate on the analytical chart, giving proper credit, of course, to the source. Some notations may be made in the side margins, opposite the text itself, the exact word or phrase of which may be identified by an arrow.

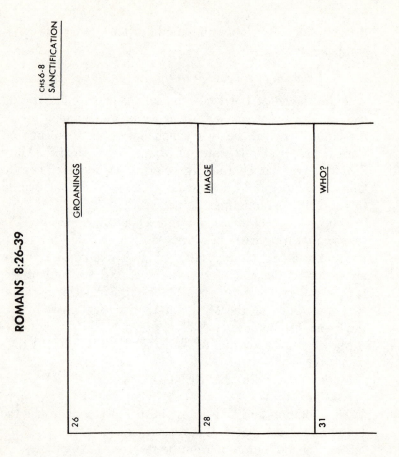

39

EARLY STAGE OF CHART

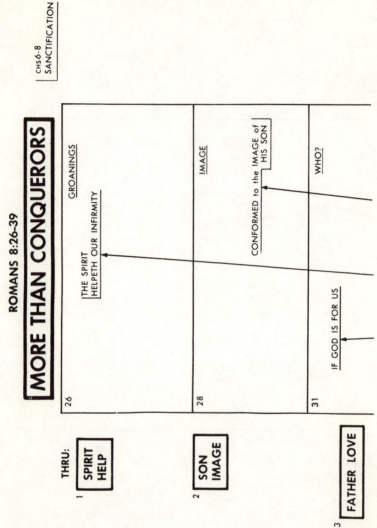

ROMANS 8:26-39

MORE THAN CONQUERORS

chs 6-8 SANCTIFICATION

THRU:

1 SPIRIT HELP

2 SON IMAGE

3 FATHER LOVE

26 GROANINGS

THE SPIRIT HELPETH OUR INFIRMITY

28 IMAGE

CONFORMED to the IMAGE of HIS SON

31 WHO?

IF GOD IS FOR US

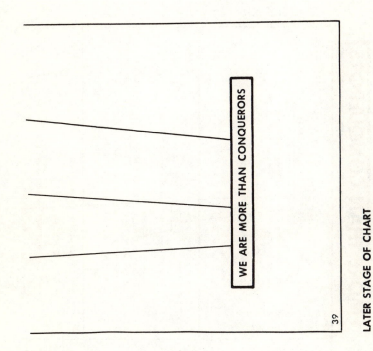

WE ARE MORE THAN CONQUERORS

39

LATER STAGE OF CHART

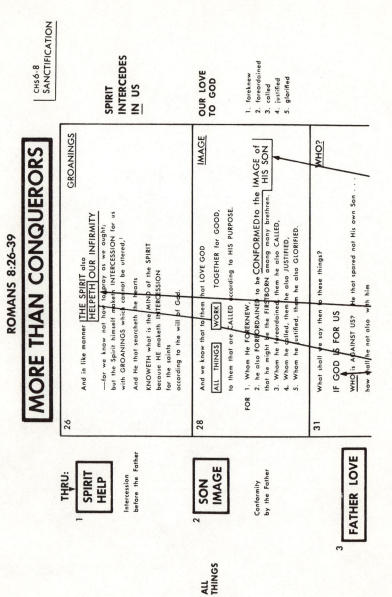

ROMANS 8:26-39

MORE THAN CONQUERORS

CHS 6-8
SANCTIFICATION

THRU:

1 SPIRIT HELP

Intercession
before the Father

26 GROANINGS

SPIRIT
INTERCEDES
IN US

And in like manner THE SPIRIT also HELPETH OUR INFIRMITY
—for we know not how to pray as we ought;
but the Spirit himself maketh INTERCESSION for us
with GROANINGS which cannot be uttered;¹
And He that searcheth the hearts
KNOWETH what is the MIND of the SPIRIT
because HE maketh INTERCESSION
for the saints
according to the will of God.

**ALL
THINGS**

2 SON IMAGE

Conformity
by the Father

28 IMAGE

OUR LOVE
TO GOD

And we know that to them that LOVE GOD
ALL THINGS WORK TOGETHER for GOOD,
to them that are CALLED according to HIS PURPOSE.

FOR 1. Whom He FOREKNEW,
2. he also FOREORDAINED to be CONFORMED to the IMAGE of HIS SON
   that he might be the FIRSTBORN among many brethren.
3. Whom he foreordained, them he also CALLED,
4. Whom he called, them he also JUSTIFIED,
5. Whom he justified, them he also GLORIFIED.

1. foreknew
2. foreordained
3. called
4. justified
5. glorified

3 FATHER LOVE

31 WHO?

What shall we say then to these things?
IF GOD IS FOR US
WHO is AGAINST US? He that spared not His own Son . . .
how shall he not also with him

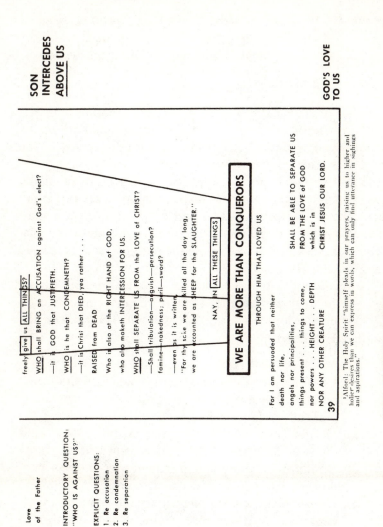

SON
INTERCEDES
ABOVE US

GOD'S LOVE
TO US

ALL
THINGS

love
of the Father

INTRODUCTORY QUESTION:
"WHO IS AGAINST US?"

EXPLICIT QUESTIONS:
1. Re accusation
2. Re condemnation
3. Re separation

ALL
THINGS

freely give us ALL THINGS?

WHO shall BRING an ACCUSATION against God's elect?

—it is GOD that JUSTIFIETH.

WHO is he that CONDEMNETH?

—it is Christ that DIED, yea rather . . .

RAISED from DEAD

Who is also at the RIGHT HAND of GOD,

who also maketh INTERCESSION FOR US.

WHO shall SEPARATE US FROM the LOVE of CHRIST?

—Shall tribulation—anguish—persecution?

famine—nakedness; peril—sword?

—even as it is written,

"For thy sake we are killed all the day long,

we are accounted as SHEEP for the SLAUGHTER."

NAY, IN ALL THESE THINGS

WE ARE MORE THAN CONQUERORS

THROUGH HIM THAT LOVED US

For I am persuaded that neither
death nor life,
angels nor principalities,
things present . . . things to come,
nor powers . . . HEIGHT . . . DEPTH
NOR ANY OTHER CREATURE
39

SHALL BE ABLE TO SEPARATE US
FROM THE LOVE OF GOD
which is in
CHRIST JESUS OUR LORD.

¹Alford: The Holy Spirit "himself pleads in our prayers, raising us to higher and holier desires than we can express in words, which can only find utterance in sighings and aspirations."

FINAL STAGE OF CHART

Example:

MARK 1:1-13

Text	*Marginal Note*
"Thou art my beloved Son, in thee I am well pleased."	order of the Greek: "Thou art the Son of me, the beloved."

Other short notations may be kept as footnotes in the bottom margin. For instance, the footnote (p. 139) to the word "dove" (Mark 1:10) reads, "in no other place in the Bible does the Spirit take on the form of a dove."

If one wishes to record a lengthy commentary or quotation which refers to any part of the analytical chart, including context and setting, it is best to use a cross-reference device and record the quote on the reverse side of the analytical chart. It is best not to use the marginal spaces for any long statements, whether one's own or another's.

In recording a topical study of another author, simply use whatever space there is in one of the margins. Refer to G. Campbell Morgan's study "HE CAME TO . . ." on the Mark 1:1-13 chart.

C. Some Dos and Don'ts

1. Do not overdo recording that which is rather obvious; do, however, give recognition to what is important, obvious or not.

2. Do not be a slave to the trite; do be original, and dig deep for many of the hidden great truths.

3. Do not overdo any one graphic device in recording; do be conservative, and aim at clarity.

4. Do not make any supplementary study more prominent than your key topical study; do remember to make the forest be seen, as well as the trees.

5. Do not read into the text; do, on the other hand, make use of a bridled imagination, especially in the narrative passages.

6. Do not overdo making isolated comments; do concentrate more on the related studies.

* * *

By now it should be evident to the student that the method of study described in the previous pages is a cumulative experience, the thoroughness of which depends on the student himself.

There are abridgements and adaptations of any method of study, and this is true of the analytical chart method. It is best not to try a shortcut, however, unless one is first acquainted with the unabridged procedure. Let each student adapt the method to his own situation. It may be remarked here that perhaps the most practical shortcut which could be engaged in is an abridgement of textual re-creation for some of the longer segments of study. Here, however, the student runs the risk of omitting some words and phrases in the text which might be crucial to his study later on. Of course, the risk diminishes with experience.

However the course may be traversed, the ultimate goal of observation is interpretation and application, which in the method described in these pages constitutes Stage Five.

V. STAGE FIVE: INTERPRETATION AND APPLICATION

As has already been remarked, observation in Bible study is with the view to interpretation and application. To observe well is to interpret well. For the analytical chart, it is advisable that most of what is recorded be observations, rather than interpretation. This is not to minimize the interpretive process, but merely to recognize that as far as the chart is concerned, most of the space is needed for all the observations which should be recorded. Actually, as has been pointed out, the student will find that the Bible passage explains much of itself by its own context; hence the emphasis in the analytical method on seeing what the Bible says. For special types of Biblical writing, such as apocalypse and prophecy, and for the complex and obscure parts of the Bible, involving also problem passages, it is wise to record—perhaps on the back side of the analytical chart— a list of one's questions and problems in the segment. Later studies and references to outside helps will probably bring answers to many of these questions. Whenever a verse from another section of the Bible will help interpret a passage in the segment, the cross-reference should be recorded on the analytical chart in the appropriate place.

If the *study* of the Bible is a continuous process, the *application* of the Bible is more so. W. P. Lockhart tells the story of the man who, on meeting his neighbor coming out of church, asked him, "Is the sermon done?" "No," was the reply, "it is preached, but it has yet to be done."

Chronologically speaking, the study of the Bible is prior to the application of the Bible. From a logical standpoint, however, the two are one, for true Bible study involves diligent response and application. Plutarch taught the parable of the man who tried to make a dead body stand upright, but who finished his labors saying: *"Deest aliquid intus"* [There's something lacking inside]. Study without response cannot bring forth life.

After studying a passage of Scripture, the student should ask himself, "How does all this apply to me?" A good reminder for this phase of one's study is to get into the habit of writing out a list of applications at the bottom margin of the analytical chart, labeling them as such. Since there will be space to list only about a half dozen of these, priority should be given to the primary.

Above all, the student should keep in mind in his total study process that he does not come to the Bible to do something to it, but to LET IT DO SOMETHING TO HIM!

CHAPTER V

PRACTICAL USES OF THE ANALYTICAL CHART

I. PERSONAL STUDY

FOR THE CHRISTIAN who wants to be engaged in a methodical program of personal Bible study, the analytical chart method is a challenging experience. Because of its flexibility, this method can be adapted to any particular situation. For instance, the student may proceed through a book of the Bible at any reasonable rate of progress. Continuity of study can be maintained despite intervening inactive study periods because there is always a clear visual record of the cumulative study for review purposes.

It is gratifying to any Bible student to have a permanent record of the hours devoted to the Bible. The analytical chart represents such a record. When kept in a loose-leaf notebook, the chart makes an attractive and valuable possession in ready-reference form.

II. SERMONIC STUDY

The analytical chart method of Bible study is a boon to the conscientious preacher. It helps him enter the pulpit with much confidence because the Biblical passage on which he is attempting to preach has become a part of him, as a result of thoroughness of analysis in which he has been engaged during the week.

It helps him see more than just the obvious in the Scriptures; he has trained himself to discover the deeper truths as well, and this his congregation expects of him.. And he

159

will preach with more power and conviction when he has discovered the Biblical truth independently of others.

It makes him essentially an expository preacher, for an expository sermon is basically the preaching of one theme as it is developed in a given passage of Scripture. In fact, the main topical study described in Stage Two (above) is practically the outlining of an expository sermon.

It disciplines him to study methodically all of the Bible, which means also that the congregation is fed a balanced diet over a period of time.

It enriches his total ministry as he is brought face to face with the varied content of the Holy Bible. His analytical studies steer him from the rut, from the trite, from the cliché, because these are not characteristic of Biblical literature.

III. TEACHING

Because of the graphic elements of the analytical chart, this method of Bible study is especially useful in teaching. In presenting a Bible passage to a class through this medium, the teacher must of course adapt the presentation to the group's age and background, length of class session, size of class and the like. It almost goes without saying that if the segment frame is sketched on a blackboard, most of the text cannot be reproduced, for want of space. Rather, key phrases are printed within the frame, as the teacher proceeds in his teaching of the lesson. The choice of the appropriate words and phrases to be used in this way requires wisdom in planning, but the impact of using the visual printed phrase at the right moment in one's teaching is tremendous. These are the truths the student will not easily forget.

A. Sunday School Class

If the Sunday school class is studying a book of the Bible, the analytical chart method is ideal for the teacher's presentation. It should be the teacher's aim to teach the members of his class how to study the Bible methodically, but it is no doubt a wise procedure to let the pupils see the teacher present his analyses from week to week throughout one entire book before he attempts to lead them to the method. Again, this project of teaching the method should be adapted to the group.

Once the pupils catch on to the method, it is amazing what interest they will take in the Bible. Bible study becomes a fascinating expedition, rather than a necessary chore.

If the teacher chooses not to teach the method to the class, he will still want to use the method himself in presenting each Bible lesson to the class. Also, if a book study is not in the curriculum at this time, the teacher may still choose to use the method for Scriptural passages from time to time as the opportunity presents itself.

B. Bible Class

For Bible classes of older age groups, the analytical chart method is equally valuable. A typical reaction to many Scripture passages is that frequently parts of the text seem unrelated to each other. Through the analytical chart method emphasis is laid upon the "togetherness" of Scriptures. The teacher in his presentation will usually want to teach the main topical study, beginning with the key center. He will aim to help the students of the class to think in terms of the three or four paragraphs of the segment rather than in terms of the twenty or twenty-five verses of the segment. Then, after the main topical study has been made, the teacher will probably want to enlarge the contents of each paragraph, as time permits.

The value of writing something of the analytical chart on the board in the process of teaching is that if a pupil fails to hear one portion of a presentation, it is there for him to see after the distraction is over.

In many adult Bible classes not too many of the class members will do a thorough work of studying the lesson before coming to class. When such is the case, it is the teacher's task to guide the students during the class session to see things in the passage, without explicitly telling the student what the observation itself is. Over a period of time the student will learn for himself how to look for things in Scripture.

The Bible class session, then, should be a discussion session, and the development of a clear abridged analytical chart on a blackboard should be a class project in which all—students and teacher—are actively engaged.

C. Midweek Bible Study

The midweek Bible study hour, which is usually held in conjunction with the prayer hour, may perhaps not be conducted as informally as a Sunday school class. The pastor or leader will undoubtedly have to do most, if not all, of the speaking. Here again, the development of an abridged analytical chart during the teaching of a passage of Scripture is invaluable.

D. College, Bible School, and Seminary Teaching

This author can testify from experience that the use of the analytical chart method on the formal education level is very rewarding. One salutary aspect of this level of education is that homework assignments are usually compulsory, so that any early reticence of the student to offer the time and toil involved in methodical study is dissolved in the actual participation in the project. This is not to imply that no one makes an analytical chart without forcing himself to do something he would rather escape, but it is to recognize that human nature and toil are not usually bedfellows from the start.

When teaching a Bible-book-study class, each consecutive segment in the Bible book will constitute the passage to be analyzed from hour to hour. Any adjustments in paragraph divisions should be given with the assignment at the previous hour. In the assignment, it is wise to give the students guiding questions—of the type that will lead him into a grasp of the more involved parts of the segment rather than questions that require a word or two for the answer. The succeeding class session is devoted to a discussion of the segment, the teacher using the board to record key phrases during the discussion and encouraging the students to offer their observations in any part of their study.

The writer, in his New Testament Survey class, has found the following procedure to be very successful. Allowing the first few weeks in the year's schedule for such items as the teaching of the analytical chart method and New Testament background material, the core of the curriculum is an alternation between analysis and synthesis. That is, for each book of the New Testament, the survey of the book (see pages 106-111) constitutes the first unit, and the analysis of a representative segment within the book constitutes the second unit. This is repeated for each book of the New Testament. The value of this procedure is that not only does the student get a view of each book as a whole, but he also gets a rather intimate glimpse of each Biblical author, what he was like, how he wrote, and what were his burdens.

In grading each analysis made by the student, this writer has used the following criteria, from a qualitative and quantitative standpoint:

1. main topical study   Maximum of 5 points
2. observations   Maximum of 5 points
3. textual re-creation   Maximum of 5 points
4. originality   Maximum of 5 points
5. clarity   Maximum of 5 points

Each analysis returned to the student has five grades on it, so that he may know in what areas he has fallen short. These five areas represent the aspects of an analytical chart which are of most importance, and the student should be continually reminded of these.

IV. RECAPITULATION

There is no substitute for methodical Bible study. If this work has succeeded in convincing the reader of this fact, it has fulfilled its primary purpose.

There are various ways to study the Bible methodically, and the analytical chart method presented in these pages is only one of them. By way of recapitulation, the following tabulation represents the major aspects of this method:

A. The Approaches

1. Inductive—arriving at the whole through discovery of the parts.
2. Deductive—proof of the parts from the truth of the whole.

B. The Recognitions

1. The Bible is literature, divinely inspired and spiritually discerned.
2. The Bible has compositional structure, or relatedness of the materials.
3. The authors applied selectivity in what was written and in what was not written, under the guidance of the Holy Spirit.
4. No Biblical statement is without context.

C. The Activities

1. Skyscraper view   (survey).
2. Microscopic view   (analysis).

D. The Main Emphases

1. Training of the eye and mind to see *what the Bible says,* as to individual facts and relatedness of these facts.

2. Graphic recording of observations, because of the advantages of visual aids.

The author has found the analytical chart method to be very fruitful in his own experience, and he is convinced that the reader's use of this method as it is described in these pages, or any equivalent adaptation of it, will fulfill the specifications of sound, scholarly, and consecrated Bible study.[1]

❖ ❖ ❖

In all your studying, study *the Bible!* Here, "there is no mere once-upon-a-time but a now, no simple yesterday but a today, no mere concern with the beyond but a God-permeated interest with this life."[2]

Read the Bible. *Study* the Bible. *Methodically study* the Bible. *Know* the Bible. And *live* the Bible, God's Book of Life and Living for all mankind.

[1]Partially completed analytical charts appear from time to time in the author's Bible Self-Study Guide series (Moody Press). Also this method is thoroughly applied in *Acts: An Independent Study* (Moody Press, 1973).

[2]Erich Sauer, *From Eternity to Eternity* (London: The Paternoster Press, 1954), p. 134.

APPENDIX I

A. A Suggested Program of Study

It is obvious that for any method of study there are some parts of the Bible which are more difficult to study than others. The beginner in the analytical chart method of study would do well to avoid the more difficult sections of the Bible while he is learning the method.

The Gospel of Mark is usually recommended as the book to be studied first, using the inductive method. The following list represents a good sequence of studies, involving variety of content and presenting fewer difficulties to the beginner in the method:

1. Mark   (narrative)
2. John   (doctrine and narrative)
3. I John   (doctrine)
4. Psalms   (poetry)
5. Nehemiah   (historical)
6. Isaiah   (prophecy)

When the student has analyzed at least a fair number of passages in these six books, he will have become acquainted with a representative cross-section of Biblical literature and can proceed to any other book with a minimum of adjustment.

Segment divisions for the above-named books are given below. Paragraph divisions for each of these segments are easily obtained from any one of, or a combination of, the following versions:

American Standard
Revised Standard
Berkeley
New International Version

B. Identification of Study Segments for the Above-named Books

On the following pages is presented a list of suggested units of study, or segments, for each of the above-named books. The segments have been made of suitable length for the analytical chart method. An abridged survey chart of each of the books is also given for the purpose of orientation, as well as to justify some segment divisions which do not concur with chapter divisions. Regarding survey study, however, the student is urged to make his own original study, as suggested in Chapter III, and to use the charts of this appendix merely as guides.

This writer recognizes that the beginning and ending locations of some units of study are not agreed upon by all Bible students. This is accounted for by the fact that some locations are arbitrary, some depend on an interpretation, and some are due to differing survey outlines. However, in most cases the disagreements are minor, as far as analysis is concerned.

In most cases, the length of the segment has been kept to under twenty-five verses in order that most of the text may be recorded on the analytical chart. The ideal length ranges from fifteen to twenty verses, and this has been followed wherever possible. The student may purposely choose to combine two segments into one study in order to include a broader scope in his study. This may be done with good advantage, though the analysis of details and textual re-creation are understandably jeopardized, in proportion.

Regarding other books of the Bible, the lengths of study segments may at times far exceed the normal length. For example, Numbers 26:1-65 may be kept as one segment rather than three, simply because, from a practical stand-

point, its census listing does not demand three studies by
the analytical chart method. Tabulations in some of the
I Chronicles passages, and the leviathan theme of Job 41,
represent segments which would be made long because of
sameness of content. The one consistent rule which should
be followed in determining the lengths of study passages
for the analytical chart method is that of *practicality*.

MARK

PROCLAMATION				WHO AM I?	PASSION		
1:1	4:1	6:1	7:1	8:27	8:31	9:30	11:1
POPULARITY AND OPPOSITION	WORDS & WORKS	NAZARETH	OVER THE BORDER	CRISIS POINT	CRISIS WEEK	TO JERUSALEM	PASSION WEEK

1:1-13	6:1-13; 14-29	11:1-19; 20-33
14-34	6:30-44; 45-56	12:1-27
35-45	7:1-23	28-44
2:1-17	24-37	13:1-23
2:18—3:6	8:1-26	24-37
3:7-19a	8:27—9:1	14:1-25
19b-35	9:2-13; 14-29	26-52
4:1-20	9:30-42; 43-50	53-72
21-41	10:1-16	15:1-21
5:1-20	17-31; 32-45	22-47
21-43	46-52	16:1-20

JOHN

PUBLIC MINISTRY: SIGNS WROUGHT		PRIVATE MINISTRY: SELF REVEALED			
1	5	12:36b	18	20	21
ANNOUNCEMENT	ELABORATION & CONFLICT	DISCOURSE & PRAYER	CRUCIFIXION	RESURRECTION	

1:1-18	7:1-24	13:1-20
19-39	25-52	21-38
40-51	7:53—8:11	14:1-31
2:1-12; 13-25	8:12-30	15:1-11
3:1-21	31-59	12-27
22-36	9:1-12	16:1-16
4:1-26	13-34; 35-41	17-33
27-42	10:1-21	17:1-26
43-54	10:22-42	18:1-27
5:1-18	11:1-16	28-40
19-29	17-44	19:1-22
30-47	45-53; 54-57	23-42
6:1-21	12:1-22	20:1-18
22-40	23-36a	19-31
41-51	36b-50	21:1-14
52-71		15-23; (24, 25)

I JOHN

GOD IS LIGHT	GOD IS LOVE	
1	3	5
"IF WE WALK IN LIGHT"	"WE HAVE FELLOWSHIP ONE WITH ANOTHER"	

1:1-10	3:1-24
2:1-17	4:1-21
18-29	5:1-12; 13-21

PSALMS

(No topical sequence, though each book has been compared with those of Pentateuch)					
1	42	73	90	106	150
BOOK I	BOOK II	BOOK III	BOOK IV	BOOK V	

The majority of the chapters of the Psalms are of segment length. The following list, representing the longer Psalms, presents recommended units of study for these Psalms.

18:1-19	69:1-18	105:1-11
20-30	19-36	12-36
31-50	71:1-16	37-45
22:1-18; 19-31	17-24	106:1-15
31:1-18	78:1-20	16-39
19-24	21-39	40-48
35:1-18	40-55	107:1-22
19-28	56-72	23-43
37:1-17	89:1-18	109:1-19
18-29	19-37	20-31
30-40	38-52	118:1-14
44:1-8	102:1-17; 18-28	15-29
9-26	104:1-23	119: (each 8 verses)
68:1-20	24-35	139:1-18; 19-24
21-35		

NEHEMIAH

REBUILDING THE WALLS			RELIGIOUS REFORMS			
1	3	7	8	11	12:27	13
PLAN AND PREPARATION	CONSTRUCTION	CENSUS	RENEWAL of COVENANT	PEOPLE SURVEY	DEDICATION	

1:1-11	7:1-73a	11:1-36
2:1-20	7:73b—8:18	12:1-30
3:1-32	9:1-5	31-47
4:1-23	6-31	13:1-14
5:1-19	32-38	15-31
6:1-19	10:1-39	

ISAIAH

HOLINESS	RIGHTEOUSNESS		JUSTICE	ORIGINS of GRACE	WORKINGS of GRACE	GLORIES of GRACE	
1	13	24	36	40	49	60	66
EXHORTATIONS & WARNINGS	PROPHECIES RE SURROUNDING NATIONS	PROMISES AND WOES	CAPTIVITY	DELIVERANCE—FUTURE GLORIES			

1:1-9	24:1-23	9-20
10-20	25:1-12	21-28
21-31	26:1-21	45:1-13
2:1-21	27:1-13	14-25
2:22—3:15	28:1-13	46:1-13
3:16—4:1	14-29	47:1-15
4:2-6	29:1-12	48:1-16
5:1-17	13-24	17-22
18-30	30:1-18	49:1-13
6:1-13	19-33	14-26
7:1-25	31:1-9	50:1-11
8:1-22	32:1-20	51:1-11
9:1-21	33:1-12	12-23
10:1-19	13-24	52:1-15
20-34	34:1-17	53:1-12
11:1-16	35:1-10	54:1-17
12:1-6	36:1-22	55:1-13
13:1-22	37:1-20	56:1-12
14:1-21	21-38	57:1-21
22-32	38:1-22	58:1-14
15:1-9	39:1-8	59:1-21
16:1-14	40:1-11	60:1-22
17:1-14	12-31	61:1-11
18:1-7	41:1-13	62:1-12
19:1-17	14-29	63:1-19
18-25	42:1-9	64:1-12
20:1-6	10-25	65:1-16
21:1-17	43:1-13	17-25
22:1-25	14-28	66:1-14
23:1-18	44:1-8	15-24

APPENDIX II

The following story of a student's crisis experience in method under the great scientist and teacher, Professor J. Louis Agassiz, has become a classic in introducing the fundamentals of *original firsthand study*. The same fundamentals apply to Bible study.

THE STUDENT, THE FISH, AND AGASSIZ

By the Student

It was more than fifteen years ago that I entered the laboratory of Professor Agassiz, and told him I had enrolled my name in the scientific school as a student of natural history. He asked me a few questions about my object in coming, my antecedents generally, the mode in which I afterwards proposed to use the knowledge I might acquire, and finally, whether I wished to study any special branch. To the latter I replied that while I wished to be well grounded in all departments of zoology, I purposed to devote myself specially to insects.

"When do you wish to begin?" he asked.

"Now," I replied.

This seemed to please him, and with an energetic "Very well," he reached from a shelf a huge jar of specimens in yellow alcohol.

"Take this fish," said he, "and look at it; we call it a Hae-mulon [pronounced Hem-yú lon]; by and by I will ask what you have seen."

With that he left me, but in a moment returned with explicit instructions as to the care of the object entrusted to me.

"No man is fit to be a naturalist," said he, "who does not know how to take care of specimens."

I was to keep the fish before me in a tin tray, and occasionally moisten the surface with alcohol from the jar, always taking care to replace the stopper tightly. Those were not the days of ground glass stoppers, and elegantly shaped exhibition jars; all the old students will recall the huge, neckless glass bottles with their leaky, wax-besmeared corks half eaten by insects and begrimed with cellar dust. Entomology was a cleaner science than ichthyology, but the example of the professor, who had unhesitatingly plunged to the bottom of the jar to produce the fish, was infectious; and though this alcohol had "a very ancient and fishlike smell," I really dared not show any aversion within these sacred precincts, and treated the alcohol as though it were pure water. Still I was conscious of a passing feeling of disappointment, for gazing at a fish did not commend itself to an ardent entomologist. My friends at home, too, were annoyed, when they discovered that no amount of eau de cologne would drown the perfume which haunted me like a shadow.

In ten minutes I had seen all that could be seen in that fish, and started in search of the professor, who had, however, left the museum; and when I returned, after lingering over some of the odd animals stored in the upper apartment, my specimen was dry all over. I dashed the fluid over the fish as if to resuscitate it from a fainting-fit, and looked with anxiety for a return of the normal, sloppy appearance. This little excitement over, nothing was to be done but return to a steadfast gaze at my mute companion. Half an hour passed, an hour, another hour; the fish began to look loathsome. I turned it over and around; looked it in the face—ghastly; from behind, beneath, above, sideways, at a three-quarters' view—just as ghastly. I was in despair; at an early hour I concluded that lunch was necessary; so, with infinite relief, the fish was carefully replaced in the jar, and for an hour I was free.

On my return, I learned that Professor Agassiz had been at the museum, but had gone and would not return for several hours. My fellow students were too busy to be disturbed by continued conversation. Slowly I drew forth that hideous fish, and with a feeling of desperation again looked at it. I might not use a magnifying glass; instruments of all kinds were interdicted. My two hands, my two eyes, and the fish; it seemed a most limited field. I pushed my finger down its throat to feel how sharp its teeth were. I began to count the scales in the different rows until I was convinced that that was nonsense. At last a happy thought struck me—I would draw the fish; and now with surprise I began to discover new features in the creature. Just then the professor returned.

"That is right," said he; "a pencil is one of the best of eyes. I am glad to notice, too, that you keep your specimen wet and your bottle corked."

With these encouraging words he added,—

"Well, what is it like?"

He listened attentively to my brief rehearsal of the structure of parts whose names were still unknown to me: the fringed gill—arches and movable operculum; the pores of the head, fleshy lips, and lidless eyes; the lateral line, the spinous fin, and forked tail; the compressed and arched body. When I had finished, he waited as if expecting more, and then, with an air of disappointment,—

"You have not looked very carefully; why," he continued, more earnestly, "you haven't seen one of the most conspicuous features of the animal, which is as plainly before your eyes as the fish itself; look again, look again!" and he left me to my misery.

I was piqued; I was mortified. Still more of that wretched fish! But now I set myself to my task with a will, and discovered one new thing after another, until I saw how just the professor's criticism had been. The afternoon passed quickly, and when, towards its close, the professor inquired,—

"Do you see it yet?"

"No," I replied, "I am certain I do not, but I see how little I saw before."

"That is next best," said he earnestly, "but I won't hear you now; put away your fish and go home; perhaps you will be ready with a better answer in the morning. I will examine you before you look at the fish."

This was disconcerting; not only must I think of my fish all night, studying, without the object before me, what this unknown but most visible feature might be; but also, without reviewing my new discoveries, I must give an exact account of them the next day. I had a bad memory; so I walked home by Charles River in a distracted state, with my two perplexities.

The cordial greeting from the professor the next morning was reassuring; here was a man who seemed to be quite as anxious as I that I should see for myself what he saw.

"Do you perhaps mean," I asked, "that the fish has symmetrical sides with paired organs?"

His thoroughly pleased, "Of course, of course!" repaid the wakeful hours of the previous night. After he had discoursed most happily and enthusiastically—as he always did—upon the importance of this point, I ventured to ask what I should do next.

"Oh, look at your fish!" he said, and left me again to my own devices. In a little more than an hour he returned and heard my new catalogue.

"That is good, that is good!" he repeated, "but that is not all; go on." And so, for three long days, he placed that fish before my eyes, forbidding me to look at anything else, or to use any artificial aid. "Look, look, look," was his repeated injunction.

This was the best entomological lesson I ever had—a lesson whose influence has extended to the details of every subsequent study; a legacy the professor has left to me, as he has left it to many others, of inestimable value, which we could not buy, with which we cannot part.

A year afterward, some of us were amusing ourselves with chalking outlandish beasts upon the museum blackboard. We drew prancing star-fishes; frogs in mortal combat; hydra-headed worms; stately craw-fishes, standing on their tails, bearing aloft umbrellas; and grotesque fishes, with gaping mouths and staring eyes. The professor came in shortly after, and was as amused as any, at our experiments. He looked at the fishes.

"Haemulons, every one of them," he said. "Mr. ——— drew them."

True; and to this day, if I attempt a fish, I can draw nothing but Haemulons.

The fourth day, a second fish of the same group was placed beside the first, and I was bidden to point out the resemblances and differences between the two; another and another followed, until the entire family lay before me, and a whole legion of jars covered the table and surrounding shelves; the odor had become a pleasant perfume; and even now, the sight of an old, six-inch, worm-eaten cork brings fragrant memories!

The whole group of Haemulons was thus brought in review; and, whether engaged upon the dissection of the internal organs, the preparation and examination of the bony framework, or the description of the various parts, Agassiz's training in the method of observing facts and their orderly arrangement was ever accompanied by the urgent exhortation not to be content with them.

"Facts are stupid things," he would say, "until brought into connection with some general law."

At the end of eight months, it was almost with reluctance that I left these friends and turned to insects; but what I had gained by this outside experience has been of greater value than years of later investigation in my favorite groups.

QUESTIONS

How carefully did you read this Agassiz story? See how many of the following questions you can answer without rereading the story.

1. The student first felt he had seen all there was to see after he had spent how much time looking at the specimen?

2. Was the student allowed to use various instruments for his study?

3. What did the student do which brought on his comment, "Now with surprise I began to discover new features. . . ."

4. Complete this statement by Agassiz: "A pencil is one of _____
   _____."

5. How many days did the student spend examining the haemulon before studying a second fish?

Make a list of various applications to Bible study which can be derived from this story. Include the following areas:

1. desire to learn	6. outside helps
2. time	7. study of structure
3. methodical procedures	8. study of context
4. recording observations	9. looking for highlights
5. concentration	10. the lasting impressions

From *American Poems* (3d ed.; Boston: Houghton, Osgood and Co., 1879), pp. 450-54. This essay first appeared in *Every Saturday*, XVI (Apr. 4, 1874), 369-70, under the title "In the Laboratory With Agassiz, By a former pupil."

GLOSSARY

ANALYTICAL CHART—A diagram of a segment of a Biblical text, with marginal notations by the student involving analytical and synthetical observations, interpretations, outlines and various other expansions. 76

ANALYTICAL METHOD—Exact, minute, and comprehensive study of all the parts of a unit of study and of their relationships. 46

ATMOSPHERE—The tone of a passage of Scripture, as indicated by either the author's words per se or the things (actions, reactions, etc.) represented by the words. 52

BOOK SURVEY STUDY—An overall "skyscraper" view of a book of the Bible without going into the details of its individual parts. This study seeks to discover the broad relationships of the various larger parts and, therefore, the unity of the whole. 106

CHAPTER TITLE—A picturesque word or short phrase taken from the chapter itself, which is merely a *clue* to the general contents of the chapter. 108

COMPOSITIONAL LAW—A pattern within an author's work whereby an impression is transmitted in a harmonious manner from the whole via the parts. (See definitions of individual laws, pp. 39 ff.) 38

CONTENT—The material, or "stuff" of words and thoughts in the Bible, or in a part thereof. 29

CORE—The combination of main subject, main verb, and main object in a sentence. 57

CROSS-REFERENCE STUDY—Reference to other verses in the Bible for the light they throw on the interpretation of the particular verse(s) under study. 64

DEDUCTIVE METHOD—Proceeding from the whole (system or conclusions) to the parts, with the aim of proving, confirming, and demonstrating. 46

179

EXEGESIS—The determining of the full meaning of a Biblical word or phrase.

EXPOSITORY SERMON—A Bible-study sermon which develops one theme in a given passage of Scripture (usually more than a few verses), allowing the passage's parts and the relations between the parts to expound this particular theme. 160

EXTRA-BIBLICAL—That which is outside of the Bible itself (e.g., a secular source of information).

FIGURATIVE TERM—A Biblical term intended to be interpreted as a representation of or likeness to its object rather than to be interpreted literally. 67

HERMENEUTICS—The science and art of interpretation. 73

HIGHER CRITICISM—That field of Biblically related studies which seeks to determine such facts as the date, authorship, backgrounds, and composition of the Scriptures. 113

HOMILETICS—The art of construction and delivery of a sermon. In practical usage it usually refers only to the construction of a sermon.

INDEPENDENT BIBLE STUDY—Individual Bible study, mainly of an original character, where most of the recourse and reference to outside helps is made in the later stages of one's study. 15

INDUCTIVE METHOD—Proceeding objectively from the parts to the whole, seeking to be informed and impressed by letting the facts speak for themselves. 44

KEY CENTER—A word or phrase within a segment which is chosen to represent the common theme of a topical study developed from paragraph to paragraph in that segment. 122

LAW OF COMPOSITION—See Compositional Law.

LITERAL TERM—A Biblical term intended to be interpreted in the precise sense of the word, and not figuratively. 67

LOWER CRITICISM—That discipline of professional study which seeks to determine as accurately as possible what the *original* text of the Scriptures must have been.

MASTER STUDY TITLE.—The title of the main topical study made on the analytical chart, to which paragraph points are shown to relate. This master title is not the same as chapter title. 124

PARAGRAPH—A group of sentences conveying one primary thought.

PARAGRAPH POINTS—The subpoints of a main topical study made on an analytical chart. There is usually one point for each paragraph. 124

PARAGRAPH TITLE—A picturesque word or short phrase taken from the paragraph itself which is merely a *clue* to the general contents of the paragraph. 116

RE-CREATION—Reproduction of the author's intents, usually in an interpretative and free form. See Textual Re-Creation. 47

ROUTINE TERMS—Biblical words and phrases within a sentence which are not weighty or crucial (see Strong Terms) but function in such capacities as grammatical connectives ("and") and ordinary narration (e.g., "he said"). 66

SEGMENT—A compositional unit of study, approximately the length of an average chapter, comprising two or more paragraphs. 57

SKYSCRAPER VIEW—The large overall view. See Book Survey Study.

STRATEGIC CENTER—The key center of a Biblical passage or book about which the message of the passage or book is seen to move. 110

STRONG TERMS—Biblical words and phrases within a sentence which are weighty, such as the descriptive, suggestive or theological, as distinguished from the ordinary and routine words within that sentence. 66

STRUCTURE—The sum total of those things in a Biblical passage or book which gives it unity or togetherness, and which marks it as a compositional work. 31

SURVEY STUDY—See Book Survey Study.

TEXTUAL CRITICISM—see Lower Criticism.

TEXTUAL RE-CREATION—Interpretive recasting, by printing, of the exact text of a Biblical passage, using various devices (grammatical diagramming, accentuations, etc.) to reflect the author's emphasis, tone, thought process, etc. 126 ff.

BIBLIOGRAPHY

Adler, Mortimer J. *How to Read A Book.* New York: Simon and Schuster, Inc. Pub., 1940.

Allis, Oswald T. *The Five Books of Moses.* 2d ed., Philadelphia: The Presbyterian and Reformed Publishing Co., 1949.

———. *The Unity of Isaiah.* Philadelphia: The Presbyterian and Reformed Publishing Co., 1950.

The Amplified New Testament. Grand Rapids: Zondervan Publishing House, 1958.

Blackwood, Andrew W. "Giving Christ the Place of Honor," *Christianity Today,* IV, 6-9 (January 18, 1960).

Bruce, F. F. *The Acts of the Apostles.* Chicago: The Inter-Varsity Christian Fellowship, 1952.

———. *The Books and the Parchments.* 3d ed., Westwood, N.J.: Fleming and H. Revell Co., 1963.

———. *Commentary on the Book of the Acts.* Grand Rapids: Wm. B. Eerdmans Publishing Co., 1954.

Culver, Robert D. *Daniel and the Latter Days.* Westwood, N.J.: Fleming H. Revell Co., 1954.

Dana, H. E. and Mantey, Julius R. *A Manual Grammar of the Greek New Testament.* New York: The Macmillan Co., 1950.

Eberhardt, Charles. *The Bible in the Making of Ministers.* New York: Association Press, 1949.

Ellis, Havelock. *Impressions and Comments.* Boston: Houghton Mifflin Co., 1929.

Gettys, Joseph M. *Teaching Pupils How to Study the Bible.* Richmond: John Knox Press, 1950.

Girdlestone, Robert Baker. *Synonyms of the Old Testament.* Grand Rapids: Wm. B. Eerdmans Publishing Co., 1953.

Goodspeed, Edgar J., translator. *New Testament.* Chicago: University of Chicago Press, 1923.

The Holy Bible. The Berkeley Version. Grand Rapids: Zondervan Publishing House, 1959.

——. Revised Standard Version. New York: Thomas Nelson and Sons, 1952.

——. Standard Edition. New York: Thomas Nelson and Sons, 1901.

——. Westminster Study Edition. Philadelphia: The Westminster Press, 1948.

Harrison, Everett F. and Pfeiffer, Charles F. *Wycliffe Bible Commentary.* Chicago: Moody Press, 1962.

Hodge, Charles. *Commentary on the Epistle to the Romans.* Grand Rapids: Wm. B. Eerdmans Publishing Co., 1950.

Jamieson, Robert, Fausset, A. R., and Brown, David. *Commentary on the Whole Bible.* Grand Rapids: Zondervan Publishing House, n.d.

Jowett, J. H. *Brooks by the Traveller's Way.* New York: George H. Doran Co., n.d.

Keil, C. F. and Delitzsch, F. *Biblical Commentary on the Old Testament.* 25 vols. Grand Rapids: W. B. Eerdmans Publishing Co., 1949.

Kerr, John H. *An Introduction to the Study of the Books of the New Testament.* New York: Fleming H. Revell Co., 1931.

Kuist, Howard Tillman. *These Words Upon Thy Heart.* Richmond: John Knox Press, 1947.

Lange, John Peter. *Commentary on the Holy Scriptures.* 24 vols. Grand Rapids: Zondervan Publishing House, n.d.

——. *Commentary on Proverbs.* Grand Rapids: Zondervan Publishing House, n.d.

Leighton, John A. *The Field of Philosophy.* New York: Appleton-Century-Crofts, Inc., 1930.

Logsdon, S. Franklin. *Thou Art My Portion.* Grand Rapids: Zondervan Publishing House, 1956.

Moffatt, James, translator. *The Bible, A New Translation.* New York: Harper and Brothers, Publishers, 1922.

Morgan, G. Campbell. *The Gospel According to Mark.* New York: Fleming H. Revell Company, 1927.

Moulton, Richard G. *The Literary Study of the Bible.* London: Ibisler and Co., Ltd., 1905.

———. *A Short Introduction to the Literature of the Bible*. Boston: D. C. Heath and Co., Publishers, 1909.

Murray, Andrew. *With Christ in the School of Prayer*. New York: Fleming H. Revell Co., n.d.

Newell, William R. *Romans*. Chicago: Moody Press, 1948.

The New English Bible. Cambridge: Cambridge University Press, and New York: Oxford University Press, 1961.

Phillips, J. B. *Letters to Young Churches*. New York: The Macmillan Company, 1950.

———. *The New Testament in Modern English*. New York: The Macmillan Company, 1953.

Ramm, Bernard. *Protestant Biblical Interpretation*. rev. ed., Boston: W. A. Wilde Co., 1956.

Robertson, A. T. *Word Pictures in the New Testament*. New York: Harper and Brothers, Publishers, 1930.

Sauer, Erich. *From Eternity to Eternity*. London: The Paternoster Press, 1954.

Tenney, Merrill C. *The Genius of the Gospels*. Grand Rapids: Wm. B. Eerdmans Publishing Co., 1951.

———. *Interpreting Revelation*. Grand Rapids: Wm. B. Eerdmans Publishing Co., 1957.

———. *John: The Gospel of Belief*. Grand Rapids: Wm. B. Eerdmans Publishing Co., 1948.

———. *The New Testament*. Grand Rapids: Wm. B. Eerdmans Publishing Co., 1955.

Terry, Milton. *Biblical Hermeneutics*. Grand Rapids: Zondervan Publishing House, n.d.

Toynbee, Arnold J. *A Study of History*. London: Oxford University Press, 1954.

Traina, Robert. *Methodical Bible Study*. Privately published, 1952.

Trench, Richard C. *Notes on the Parables of Our Lord*. London: Kegan Paul, Trench, and Co., 1889.

Unger, Merrill F. *Introductory Guide to the Old Testament*. Grand Rapids: Zondervan Publishing House, 1951.

Vincent, Marvin R. *Word Studies in the New Testament*. Grand Rapids: Wm. B. Eerdmans Publishing Co., 1946.

Vine, W. E. *An Expository Dictionary of New Testament Words.* Westwood, N.J.: Fleming H. Revell Co., 1961.

Vos, Howard. *Effective Bible Study.* 2d ed., Grand Rapids: Zondervan Publishing House, 1956.

Wagner, Don M. *The Expository Method of G. Campbell Morgan.* Westwood, N.J.: Fleming H. Revell Co., 1957.

Weeks, Edward. "The Peripatetic Reviewer," *The Atlantic Monthly,* Vol. 185 (June, 1950).

Westcott, B. F. *St. Paul's Epistle to the Ephesians.* Grand Rapids: Wm. B. Eerdmans Publishing Co., 1950.

Weymouth, Richard F. *The New Testament in Modern Speech.* 5th ed.; New York: Harper and Brothers, 1929.

Williams, Charles B. *The New Testament in the Language of the People.* Chicago: Moody Press, 1952.

Wuest, Kenneth S. *Acts Through Ephesians.* Grand Rapids: Wm. B. Eerdmans Publishing Company, 1958.

———. *The Gospels.* Grand Rapids: Wm. B. Eerdmans Publishing Company, 1956.

———. *Philippians Through Revelation.* Grand Rapids: Wm. B. Eerdmans Publishing Company, 1959.

GENERAL INDEX